MASTERING *the* ART
of JAPANESE HOME COOKING

MASTERING *the* ART
of
JAPANESE
HOME COOKING

MASAHARU MORIMOTO

Photography by Evan Sung

ecco

An Imprint of HarperCollins*Publishers*

Contents

INTRODUCTION *1*

The Japanese Meal: *Turning the recipes in this book into dinner* 10

DASHI
THE EASY, ESSENTIAL JAPANESE STOCK

20 Dashi: *Dried fish and kelp stock*
23 Kombu Dashi: *Kelp stock*

GOHAN
RICE

33 Hakumai: *Perfect white rice*
37 Onigiri: *Rice balls*
39 Yaki Onigiri: *Grilled rice balls*
40 Omuraisu: *Omelet with ketchup-fried rice*
43 Takikomi Gohan: *Dashi-simmered rice with vegetables*
47 Chahan: *Japanese-style fried rice*
50 Su Meshi: *Sushi rice*
53 Temaki: *Hand rolls*
     Spicy Tuna Temaki
     Ume-Shiso Temaki
     Vegetable Temaki
     California Temaki

61 Battera: *Pressed mackerel sushi*
67 Oyako Don: *Chicken and egg rice bowl*
69 Katsu Don: *Pork cutlet and egg rice bowl*
70 Suteki Don: *Steak rice bowls with spicy teriyaki sauce*
73 Tekka Don No Poke: *Hawaiian poke-style tuna rice bowl*

SUPU
SOUPS

77 Miso Shiru: *Miso soup with tofu*
78 Asari No Miso Shiru: *Miso soup with clams*
81 Tonjiru: *Hearty miso soup with pork and vegetables*
85 Tamago Supu: *Japanese egg drop soup*
87 Dango Jiru: *Japanese-style chicken and dumpling soup*
89 Dobin Mushi: *Aromatic "tea pot" soup with mushrooms, fish, and shrimp*

YAKU

TO GRILL, BROIL, AND SEAR

95 A Yakitori Party: *Grilled chicken and vegetable skewers*

98 Tsukune No Teriyaki: *Chicken meatballs with teriyaki sauce*

100 Sake Shioyaki: *Salt-grilled salmon*

102 Sakana No Misoyaki: *Grilled miso-marinated fish*

104 Nasu No Misoyaki: *Eggplant with chicken and miso sauce*

107 Tori No Teriyaki: *Chicken teriyaki*

109 Gyoza: *Pork and cabbage dumplings*

115 Tamagoyaki: *Japanese Omelet*

118 Buta No Shogayaki: *Pork belly with ginger and onions*

MUSU

TO STEAM

122 Sakana No Sakamushi: *Fish steamed in kombu with spicy soy sauce*

125 Shumai: *Japanese-style shrimp dumplings*

133 Chawanmushi: *Egg custard with shrimp, chicken, and fish*

NIRU

TO SIMMER

141 Saba No Misoni: *Mackerel simmered with miso*

145 Nitsuke: *Fish simmered with sake, soy sauce, and sugar*

146 Hambagu: *Japanese-style hamburger with tangy sauce*

150 Buta No Kakuni: *Slow-cooked pork belly with beer-teriyaki glaze*

153 Chikuzenni: *Chicken simmered with lotus root and bamboo shoot*

155 Nikujaga: *Japanese-style beef stew*

158 Hijiki: *Sweet simmered hijiki seaweed*

161 Karei Raisu: *Japanese-style curry*

166 Oden: *Japanese-style hot pot*

ITAME RU

TO STIR-FRY

171 Kinpira: *Stir-fried parsnip and carrot*

173 Yasai Itame: *Stir-fried vegetables*

174 Kaisen Yaki Udon: *Stir-fried udon noodles with seafood*

177 Yakisoba: *Stir-fried noodles with pork, cabbage, and ginger*

MEN

NOODLES

184 Kinoko Zaru Soba: *Chilled soba noodles with mushrooms*

186 Kamo Nanban Soba: *Soba noodle soup with duck and spring vegetables*

189 Homemade Udon Noodles

193 Zaru Udon: *Chilled udon noodles with scallions and ginger*

195 Nabeyaki Udon: *"Clay pot" udon noodle soup*

197 Supagetti No Teriyaki: *Chicken teriyaki spaghetti*

AGERU

TO FRY

205 Yasai Tempura: *Vegetable tempura*

208 Kaki Age: *Shrimp and vegetable fritters*

211 Kara Age: *Japanese-style fried chicken with scallion sauce*

215 Tonkatsu: *Japanese-style fried pork cutlet*

218 Menchi Katsu: *Crispy fried beef patties*

221 Kabocha Korokke: *Squash croquettes*

AE RU

TO DRESS

227 Ingen No Goma Ae: *Green beans with sesame dressing*

230 Karashi Ae: *Brussels sprouts, shrimp, and mushrooms with Japanese mustard dressing*

233 Shira Ae: *Spinach, carrot, and shiitake with tofu dressing*

235 Sumiso Ae: *Squid and scallions with miso-vinegar dressing*

TSUKERU

TO PICKLE

240 Tataki Kyuri: *Smashed cucumber pickles*

242 Shiozuke: *Salt pickles*

243 Misozuke: *Miso pickles*

246 Nukazuke: *Rice bran pickles*

Acknowledgments   251

Ingredient Glossary   253

Sources   261

Index   265

MASTERING *the* ART
of JAPANESE HOME COOKING

Introduction

Long before I was an Iron Chef with a restaurant empire
of my own, I was the young executive chef at Nobu
restaurant in New York City. Nobu Matsuhisa, the owner
and chef, served boundary-crossing Japanese food inspired
by his time in Peru. He dazzled American diners with
dishes that fused exotic-seeming elements of Japanese food
(raw fish, mysterious-sounding ingredients like *uni* and
yuzu) with the bright flavors of Latin America—chiles,
lime, and cilantro.

At the time, I was struck by the fact that perhaps his most celebrated
dish, the one that earned breathless reviews from the *New York Times*
and cost diners $25 a plate, was miso-marinated black cod. As a boy, I'd
gobbled this dish many times at the table in my family's little house in
Hiroshima prefecture. My grandmother might have used a more modest
fish than rich, silky black cod and left out the bright pink pickled ginger
shoot and drizzle of sauce that garnished the plate at Nobu. Otherwise,
hers was essentially identical.

Because Americans were unfamiliar with the dish and because it
shared a menu with all that creative fusion food, the staple of Japanese
home cooking seemed like a brilliant chef's invention. Nobu-san's real
stroke of brilliance was simply realizing how much Americans would love
the dish. The praise it inspired revealed how thrilling even the simplest
Japanese home cooking could be.

The years since then have been good ones for Japanese cuisine in
America. We've seen sushi go from exotic rarity to supermarket staple.
We've seen tempura become a household term. We've witnessed the rise
of ramen and soba and *yakitori*. The enthusiastic embrace of Japanese food

was no surprise to those of us who grew up relishing its lightness and healthfulness, its simplicity and its umami, that hard-to-describe fifth flavor that is sometimes translated as "mouth-fillingly delicious."

No question: Americans adore Japanese food. But though other cuisines—Mexican or Italian or French— are locally beloved, cooks here don't even attempt to make Japanese food at home. Why not? I have a theory: lore and mystique plague the cuisine. Americans have heard again and again that the best sushi chefs train for years before they're allowed to even touch rice or fish. They've heard tales of *kaiseki,* the elaborate parade of tiny dishes made from ingredients that might be in season for mere weeks. They've heard about the Japanese penchant for specialization: restaurants are devoted to one ingredient (like eel) or dish (like tempura), and master practitioners dedicate their lives to the craft. The takeaway: this cuisine is best left to experts. No wonder home cooks are afraid to try it!

But we Japanese chefs know a secret. The flavors that our customers adore aren't so hard to create. They exist in the incredible, underexplored world of Japanese home cooking.

It's true that I spent many years learning the intricacies of fish and rice making so my sushi would satisfy connoisseurs spending $200 on dinner. Home cooks across Japan, however, make a different kind of delicious sushi. They fold a mixture of vinegar, sugar, and salt into cooked short-grain rice and set the result on the table alongside nori (easy-to-find sheets of dried seaweed) and a modest array of vegetables or fish. The family digs in, everyone spreading the rice onto the nori, adding the filling, and rolling the package into a cylinder by hand. This is *temaki zushi,* or hand rolls. They require no special skills or equipment to make. Yet because you make them yourself, the nori stays crisp, the rice stays warm, and gummy, soggy take-out sushi rolls become a distant memory.

This is true for so many exalted dishes: they might take years of training to produce at the highest level at the most celebrated restaurants, but they require only a little know-how to become tasty, satisfying dinners at home.

The finest soba noodles, for instance, are handmade from freshly milled and meticulously polished buckwheat. Yet in Japanese homes across the globe, store-bought dried noodles make a delightful centerpiece for a simple meal served with grated radish and dipping sauce. You'll pay dearly for featherweight fried maitake mushrooms and lotus root at the finest tempura restaurants in Tokyo, where chefs create edible art with bubbling oil. Yet once you've mastered a few simple techniques, you'll impress your friends with vegetables encased in impossibly light, greaseless crunch. The now-famous black cod with miso, too, has its fussed-over versions. Yet all my grandmother did to make *misoyaki* was slather a four-ingredient marinade onto fish and broil it. Hers is still my favorite.

Ironically, it took me leaving home to experience real home cooking. I loved my mother, but she was not a good cook. She grew up wealthy, surrounded by housekeepers who cooked and cleaned for her. She barely had to put her clothes on herself. After World War II, her family lost everything. By the time she married my father and had me, she was too busy working to catch up on all the cooking experience she had missed.

The only weapon in her arsenal was soy sauce. In most households at the time, mothers used *dashi,* the simple stock made from dried fish and kelp that is the backbone of so many Japanese dishes. My mother? She tried to mimic its flavor with soy sauce mixed with water. Instead of the classic tempura sauce (a mixture of dashi, soy sauce, and sweet rice wine), she served the deep-fried vegetables with a bowl of soy sauce. Instead of the perfectly calibrated salty-sweet dipping sauce for cold soba noodles, she served a bowl of—you guessed it—soy sauce!

As a young, growing Morimoto, I didn't know any better. I was concerned only with shoveling in as much food as I could in one sitting. And perhaps because of my mother's soy sauce habit, I preferred rice to anything else. By the time I was a teenager, my dinner was a small piece of grilled fish with soy sauce and ten bowls of rice. (Keep in mind that Japanese rice bowls are small, but also that mine were always piled high!) As long as I was full, I was happy.

I was a hungry boy, because I was training every day to become a baseball player. Baseball was my first love. I was a catcher. I dreamed of being drafted by my hometown team, the Hiroshima Carps. After that, who knows? Maybe I'd play for the Yankees—or at least the Mets. I had a real chance to play professionally in Japan until I injured my shoulder and understood that I could never make it. Then my career path was clear, because I had only one other passion: sushi.

My family didn't have much money. My father was a drinker, and my home life was difficult. But a couple of times a year, all of us—my father, mother, sister, and I—would get dressed up and go out for sushi. We'd sit

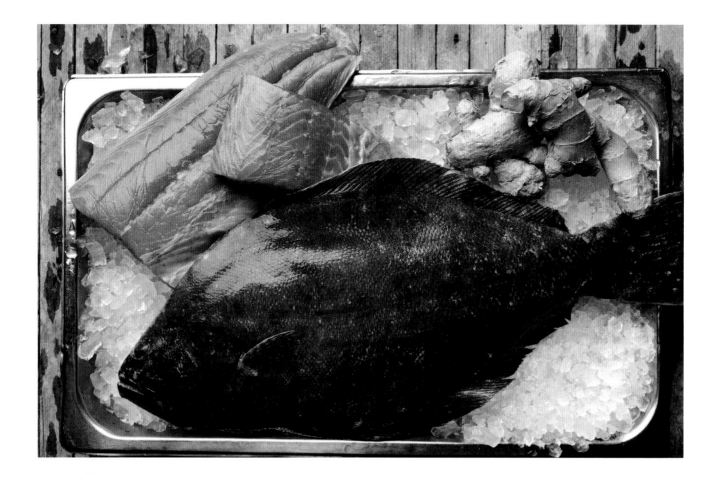

at the counter and I would stare at the sushi chefs' practiced hands as they sliced fish and swiftly formed each piece, mesmerized as if I were at a magic show. They looked very, very cool. When I missed out on my first dream, becoming one of these men, who wore clean white jackets and made families happy, came to be my new one.

So, at age eighteen, I began washing dishes at Ichiban Zushi, a restaurant in Hiroshima run by a man named Ikuo Oyama. He saw how hungry I was to learn, and I soon became his apprentice, living in a room above the restaurant and working long hours. My job began when I opened my eyes at 5 a.m. and ended when I closed them at 2 a.m.

Ichiban served sushi and made a range of food sold at a supermarket next door. Oyama-san would ultimately teach me to slice fish in the artful sushi style. But first, I had to learn to cook the supermarket food and the food that Oyama-san and his family ate for dinner—that is, many staples of Japanese home cooking.

Oyama-san's wife taught me to cook simple food the old way, how to make *kimpira* (sweet-salty simmered root vegetables), *nikujaga* (soy sauce and

sake–laced beef stew), and *korokke* (deep-fried potato croquettes). I also learned for the first time that tempura had its own umami-packed sauce. It was under her tutelage that I made my first dashi. Every morning, she and her daughter-in-law made the stock from scratch, steeping *kombu* in a pot of barely bubbling water before adding handfuls of the feathery *katsuobushi* flakes. She strained the liquid and used it in everything from miso soup to simmered fish to omelets. Though making the stock took only fifteen minutes, I didn't yet understand why they put in the effort. After all, my mother's stand-in of soy sauce mixed with water took mere seconds.

We cooked in a small room with a stainless steel counter and a few countertop burners—a far cry from the vast, gleaming kitchens of my restaurants today. I sat with the family and we all ate together. For the first time, I saw people savoring food. They talked about each dish, complimenting the flavor of a particular ingredient or noting that a dish was too salty or sweet. As they discussed the finer points of tempura and *tonkatsu,* I looked at my empty bowl and realized that I'd gulped down my food without really tasting it. From then on, I decided that learning to taste food was just as important as cooking. I began to understand why they made their own pickles—hers tasted better and cost less than those sold at the market. I got why she took the time to make the painstaking multilayered omelet called *tamagoyaki*—because its texture was like nothing else. And I finally realized why they made *dashi*—the stock that transforms something as simple as boiled spinach into the shockingly flavorful, umami-filled dish called *ohitashi*.

Soon I started making all the food sold in the supermarket, plus dinner for the family. This was a lot of work. In the little time I had between the chopping and simmering and frying, I tried to make the food as tasty as I could. My struggle was a glimpse into what home cooks—who in Japan at the time were mostly women—toiled to accomplish every day. This kind of cooking was not an art; it was a job. And it gave rise to dishes that are both delicious and easy to make.

This book is devoted to these simple and spectacular examples of Japanese home cooking. It's a catalog of ideas from Japanese grandmothers, a highlight reel that includes my favorite dishes to eat at home. It's also my attempt to hold on to some of the old ways, the ingredients and techniques that make the most delicious food. As time and technology march forward, home cooking in Japan has changed. Oyama-san's wife has since passed away. Oyama-san recently turned ninety years old. Young people are gulping, just as I used to. Quality cooking has lost out to convenience and speed. No longer does every house have a crock of rice bran pickles fermenting. The most popular food to eat at Christmastime is a bucket of fried chicken from KFC.

Not all progress is bad, of course. Today when you turn on the faucet, out comes water; when you turn on the stove, out come flames. When I was born, on the other hand, my family got water from a well and lit a fire when we wanted to cook. In the same way, I'm happy that home cooks in modern Japan and America can buy *katsuobushi* preshaved at the store. Just a few decades ago, you'd have to buy blocks of the dried, smoked, and fermented fish and shave them yourself on a *kezuriki*, a wooden device similar to a carpenter's plane. Yet we have gone too far. Nowadays many home cooks (and even many restaurants) use packaged, powdered dashi, a product made mainly of salt, sugar, and MSG. This should not be. Not only does real dashi put powdered imitators to shame—it requires just two ingredients. Instead of the hours of simmering that French stock requires, all dashi takes is a brief steeping. Why take the shortcut when the long way isn't all that long?

The good news is that cooking real Japanese food in America has never been easier. Unlike Thai or Vietnamese foods, which rely on hard-to-find fresh ingredients (Thai chiles, lemongrass, anise-scented sweet basil), Japanese home cooking owes its characteristic flavors to a half-dozen pantry ingredients. You can now find these staples on supermarket shelves

from Ann Arbor to Austin, from Seattle to Savannah, and they last indefinitely in the fridge or cupboard. This is the magic of Japanese food. You build a pantry, combine a few ingredients in the right ratios, and you're ready to cook hundreds of dishes, including (but not limited to) the recipes in this book.

It's out of hope that I named this book after Julia Child's groundbreaking *Mastering the Art of French Cooking*. Her book changed the way Americans thought about French food, igniting both passion for an unfamiliar cuisine and, perhaps more important, starting people down the path to understanding. In this book, I hope to do the same for Japanese home cooking.

Of course, this book, like Mrs. Child's, does not and could not include every dish in the Japanese grandmother's repertoire. If it did, the book might leave you feeling overwhelmed instead of inspired. I decided to limit the recipes to my true favorites, the ones I would whip up for you and your family in your kitchen if I could.

My goal is to introduce you to dishes that you've probably never tried but that I know you will adore. I also want to reacquaint you with dishes (tempura!) and sauces (teriyaki!) that have been misrepresented in bad restaurants and supermarket bottles. I want you to become a cheerleader for Japanese home cooking, and introduce your family and friends to its wonders. And so I've gone into the kitchen to make these dishes for the first time in years—my wife, Keiko, is the home cook in the Morimoto family—tinkering with them to reflect American seasonal ingredients and adding a few twists here and there. My grandmother's generation certainly did not use kale in their *ohitashi* (page 22) and would have screamed in horror to see aioli served alongside *oden* (page 166). But I am Morimoto-san, after all.

THE JAPANESE MEAL
Turning the recipes in this book into dinner

There are no laws about eating Japanese food. Even though I would not suggest, for instance, mixing wasabi and soy sauce for your sushi or spearing soba noodles with a fork and not chopsticks, you should do what you like best. That's the fun of cooking at home: your house, your rules!

Yet before you start cooking, let me tell you about how *I* would eat the food in this book. In other words, let me tell you about how a Japanese person makes different dishes into a meal at home. In general, and whether we realize it or not, Japanese people often follow the principles of *ichiju sansai,* which basically translates to "one soup and three dishes." The soup and these three dishes—usually some form of rice, protein, and vegetable—are eaten at the same time, not in courses. Each particular combination takes balance into account—balance of flavors, textures, and richness.

I hope this talk of principles and balance doesn't seem intimidating, like some art you must master, because it's not! Americans, too, achieve

balance in their food whenever they serve a salad with a steak or choose not to serve a baked potato with a bowl of pasta. The same logic applies to Japanese food, though instead of a main dish there are often several smaller dishes. Take as an example the typical Japanese breakfast: there is a bowl of miso soup, a bowl of plain rice, a piece of simply prepared fish, and pickled vegetables. The soup is nourishing and warm. The rice is starchy, slightly sweet, but mostly pleasantly bland. The fish is rich and filling. The pickles are crunchy, intensely flavored, and light. A bite of one dish makes you crave a bite of the others. You eat and feel satisfied, not stuffed.

These general categories—soup, starch, protein, vegetable—can be mixed and matched to your liking. Instead of miso soup, you could whip up Japanese egg drop soup. Instead of fish, perhaps you'd like chicken teriyaki or *tamagoyaki* (the Japanese omelet). Instead of plain rice, you might choose *onigiri* (rice balls) or *takikomi gohan* (rice cooked in dashi with vegetables). Instead of pickles, you might make green beans with sesame dressing or sweet-salty simmered *hijiki,* a dark, nutritious sea vegetable. Japanese cooks instinctively make meals from dishes made with different cooking methods—a fried dish might share the table with a simmered dish, a pickled one, and a dressed one. That's one reason I divided the book's recipes into chapters based on cooking method and starch type. Take one recipe from each of three or four chapters and there's your balanced meal.

Meals can certainly be more elaborate or less. Instead of three dishes, you could add a few extra—maybe *ohitashi* (dashi-marinated kale) and *gyoza* (pork and cabbage dumplings). Instead of separate protein and vegetable dishes, you could serve one, like *chikuzenni,* that contains both. And while you don't *need* rice to make a meal, I can't imagine one without it. In fact, much of the food in the Japanese repertoire only makes sense when you imagine a bowl of rice beside it. Dishes that might seem too intensely flavored on their own—eggplant doused in a rich, salty miso sauce, for example, or fish simmered with soy, sake, and sugar—are perfect with the steaming, mild grains to soak up all that deliciousness.

Of course, I don't expect any home cook to prepare four separate recipes a night. Not even Grandma does that! Instead she always has a few dishes in the fridge—typically simple foods that are boldly seasoned and taste just as good, if not better, a few days after they're made. This is true of *nikujaga* (Japanese beef stew), *kinpira* (stir-fried parsnip and carrot), *hijiki,* pickles, and many more dishes. And it means that you can make just one new dish on a night and still serve a complete, impressive Japanese dinner.

And yes, there are many exceptions to the *ichiju sansai* meal. Just as I sometimes grab a burger for lunch, I also fill my belly with the one-dish meal called *donburi*—a bowl of rice topped with chicken and egg, beef, or raw tuna—or slurp down a plate of chilled udon noodles with dipping sauce. Sure, my wife might urge me to eat some vegetables alongside, but I admit I don't always. Use common sense: if your protein is *kakuni* (simmered pork belly), you might not want to pair it with *tonkatsu* (deep-fried pork cutlet). The key word is *might*—because remember, your house, your rules.

DASHI だし

The easy, essential Japanese stock

Meet Japanese cuisine's secret weapon: dashi. Whenever a simple Japanese dish—a bowl of soup, a small pile of boiled spinach, a jumble of egg and chicken over rice—shocks you with its depth of flavor, dashi is to thank.

Similar to the role chicken and veal stocks play in Western cuisines, dashi provides the backbone of flavor that helps other ingredients stand tall. Yet while meat stock is thick and intense, a punch to the mouth, dashi is light and clean in body and flavor, blowing a subtle ocean breeze into everything it touches. Dashi also makes classic French stock seem like brain surgery. Instead of hours of simmering, dashi requires just fifteen minutes of steeping. Instead of bones, vegetables, and herbs, dashi requires just two ingredients. Despite this, I'm sad to say that many cooks in Japan nowadays no longer make dashi, relying instead on a powdered product, the Japanese equivalent of chicken bouillon. I'm begging you—don't make this mistake.

Dashi begins with kombu, a type of kelp harvested from the cold waters around Hokkaido, Japan's northern island, that's sun-dried, cut, and sold in blackish-green ribbons. The most elemental version of dashi is kombu steeped in water. That's it. Frequently, however, kombu joins forces with *katsuobushi,* skipjack tuna or bonito that has been dried, smoked, and often fermented. In the old days, all cooks bought the fish in blocks that resembled petrified wood and shaved them by hand into fine, feather-like flakes. (Today, most buy preshaved *katsuobushi,* one modern convenience I can get behind.) Kombu contributes a briny, green flavor, while *katsuobushi* adds a subtle sweetness and smokiness. And both ingredients add umami. In case you're not familiar, umami is a concept coined by a Japanese scientist who in the early 1900s did research in an attempt to explain why dashi tastes so good. It turns out that kombu and *katsuobushi* contain a substance called glutamic acid— so do other umami-giving ingredients, from tomatoes and Parmesan to mushrooms and miso—that produces a wonderful sensation best translated as "Wow, that's delicious!" In the past decade, umami has been recognized not just as a result of combining the four basic tastes that kids learn about in science class—sweet, sour, bitter, and salty—but as a taste of its own. Science aside, all you need to know is that whatever

THE KEYS TO MAKING DASHI AT HOME

+ Good dashi is about balance—the sea-sweetness and smokiness of the *katsuobushi,* the subtle brininess of the kombu—so measure the ingredients as precisely as possible.

+ Be vigilant: dashi takes very little time and effort, but do remember to keep an eye on the water to make sure it never fully simmers, let alone boils. This will give your dashi a sour or bitter flavor.

+ When you strain the stock during the final step of dashi making, resist the temptation to wring the *katsuobushi* to extract every last bit of liquid. A light press with a wooden spoon is sufficient—squeeze and you'll end up with sour dashi.

umami-rich dashi touches tastes even more packed with flavor than it did before.

Like many Japanese ingredients, *katsuobushi* and kombu are fetishized by the finest chefs, who pay dearly for the highest grades. And though making dashi is essentially uncomplicated, master practitioners obsess over the technique. At home, however, making dashi could not be less complicated. Its two ingredients are now widely available—at Japanese markets and online, yes, but also at many health-food stores and American supermarkets. The process is straightforward and the results are immediately rewarding. Once you have it in your arsenal, you're ready to make *ohitashi* (page 22), vegetables like spinach or kale marinated in seasoned dashi. You're minutes away from the best miso soup (page 77) you've ever tasted. You can turn ingredients as plain as egg, chicken, and rice into the sublime meal-in-a-bowl known as *oyako don* (page 67). In other words, for anyone eager to start on the recipes in this book, making dashi should be your first order of business. Your cooking will never be the same.

DASHI

Japan's legendary super-broth is the key to simple home cooking that has deep, satisfying flavor. It requires just fifteen minutes and two ingredients that last virtually forever in your pantry and are easier than ever to find. I can't think of a better use of your time than making it right away!

MAKES ABOUT 7 CUPS

Special Equipment
Cheesecloth

½ ounce kombu (dried kelp; an approximately 5 by 6-inch
   piece)
8 cups water, preferably filtered or spring water
1½ ounces bonito flakes (*katsuobushi*), about 3 cups lightly
   packed

Briefly and gently wipe the kombu with a damp towel to remove any dirt or grit, but do not scrub off the white stuff.

Combine the water and kombu in a medium pot, set over medium heat, and heat uncovered just until you see small bubbles break the surface of the water, 10 to 12 minutes. Take the pot off the heat.

Use tongs to remove and discard the kombu. Add the bonito flakes to the pot and stir gently to distribute the flakes throughout the liquid. Let the flakes steep for about 1 minute and use a spoon to skim off any white froth from the surface of the liquid. Let the flakes steep for 2 minutes more.

Line a sieve or strainer with cheesecloth or sturdy paper towels, set the sieve over a large container, and pour in the dashi. Very gently press the flakes and discard them.

If you're not using the dashi right away, let it cool to room temperature and store it in an air-tight container in the fridge for up to 4 days, or in the freezer for up to 3 months.

OHITASHI
Dashi-marinated kale

Dashi is incredibly versatile—like many stocks, it serves as the base for countless soups and adds richness and depth to stews, simmered dishes, sauces, and more. But perhaps its simplest use is as a sort of marinade for vegetables for a dish called *ohitashi*. Once they're briefly boiled and shocked in icy water, so many vegetables— from seasonal ones like asparagus and okra to the classic spinach—benefit from a bath in seasoned dashi. The technique makes the vegetable taste richer and even more like itself. Here, I use the beloved American green kale, which has a bolder flavor than spinach and makes particularly delicious, if untraditional, *ohitashi*.

SERVES 4

Kosher salt

One ½-pound bunch kale, such as curly, Russian, or Tuscan, thick bottom stems trimmed and discarded

1½ cups Dashi (dried fish and kelp stock, page 20) or Kombu Dashi (kelp stock, page 23)

1 teaspoon *usukuchi* (Japanese light-colored soy sauce)

1 teaspoon mirin (sweet rice wine)

1 heaping tablespoon bonito flakes (*katsuobushi*)

Bring a medium pot of water to a boil and add enough salt (about 1 tablespoon) so it tastes lightly salty. Prepare a medium mixing bowl full of icy water.

Bundle the kale so the stem ends are lined up. Grab the kale bundle by the leaves and submerge about 2 inches of the stems in the water. Wait 30 seconds, then add the kale to the water and stir well. Cook until the kale is fully tender but still retains some texture, 3 to 4 minutes. Use tongs to transfer the kale to the icy water, stir well, and let it fully cool. Remove the kale and firmly squeeze it to remove as much water as you can.

Combine the dashi, soy sauce, mirin, and 1 teaspoon salt in a small saucepan, set it over medium heat, and cook, stirring, just until the salt fully dissolves. Let the dashi mixture cool and pour it in a medium mixing bowl. Add the kale, breaking up the clumps, stir, and cover the bowl. Refrigerate for at least 2 hours or up to 24 hours, the longer the better.

When you're ready to eat, take the kale out of the fridge and wait about 5 minutes, so it's cool but no longer cold. Gently squeeze the kale back into the bowl, reserving the liquid. Line up the kale leaves on a cutting board and gather them into a long, tight bundle about 1½ inches high and 8 inches long. Cut it crosswise into 2-inch pieces and arrange them on a small plate. Spoon on about 3 tablespoons of the reserved liquid or more to taste. Rub the bonito flakes between dry hands to make them finer, sprinkle on top, and serve.

KOMBU DASHI

KELP STOCK

You'd think that classic dashi couldn't be simpler. After all, it's made from water and two ingredients. Yet this version, a staple of Japan's rich tradition of vegetarian cooking, manages to cut the number of ingredients in half. Kombu (dried kelp) alone infuses water with its quietly briny flavor to produce liquid umami. The result is different from the slightly sweeter, smokier dashi made with the shavings of dried fish called katsuobushi, *but it's a great alternative, whether you're making vegetarian food or you're low on* katsuobushi.

MAKES ABOUT 7½ CUPS

2 ounces kombu (dried kelp; four approximately 5 by 6-inch pieces)
8 cups water, preferably filtered or spring water

Briefly and gently wipe the kombu with a damp towel to remove any dirt or grit, but do not scrub off the white stuff.

Combine the water and kombu in a medium pot, set over medium heat, and heat uncovered just until you see small bubbles break the surface of the water, 10 to 12 minutes. Take the pot off the heat. Use tongs to remove the kombu. If there are kombu particles in your broth, set a fine-mesh sieve over a container and strain the dashi.

If you're not using the dashi right away, let it cool to room temperature and store it in an airtight container in the fridge for up to 4 days, or in the freezer for up to 3 months.

MORIMOTO MAGIC TRICK: YOU CAN MAKE KOMBU DASHI WITHOUT TURNING ON YOUR STOVE! COMBINE THE KOMBU AND WATER IN A LARGE CONTAINER, COVER TIGHTLY, AND KEEP IN THE FRIDGE FOR 12 HOURS. REMOVE THE KOMBU AND POOF—DASHI!

GOHAN

ライス

Rice

When I started working in restaurants, I was up to my elbows in rice—literally. At Ichiban in Hiroshima, I spent four years learning how to properly cook rice before my boss, Chef Ikuo Oyama, let me pick up a knife.

Each morning at Ichiban, I'd plunge my hands into a bowl of raw short-grain rice so deep that, yes, the grains nearly reached my elbows! With the bowl under running water, I'd swish the rice around, then drain the water, then swish and drain again and again until the water was no longer cloudy from the rice's starch. Once it was properly washed, I'd combine the rice with fresh water in a huge pot. The amount of water always varied, depending on the batch of dry rice, the weather, and other factors. Over time, Oyama-san taught me how to tell, simply by feeling the grains, how much to adjust the amount of water. Since this was rice for sushi, I transferred the cooked rice to a shallow wooden tub called *hangiri* and poured on a mixture of vinegar, sugar, and salt, stirring and folding with a wooden paddle. I folded very, very gently, for if I had smashed any of those fussed-over grains, Oyama-san would not have been happy.

At first, I didn't understand why I had to make rice, why I wasn't allowed to cut fish right away. As a boy, I idolized the sushi chefs working quietly and surely behind the counter at the restaurant my family visited on special occasions. So by the time I got to Ichiban, I was eager to put on a crisp white uniform and get down to the real business of sushi making. Yet the key to sushi, as Oyama-san explained, is not the fish or the forming, but the rice. "How can this be?" you might wonder. "It's just rice." Well, my friends, in Japan rice is so much more than just rice.

That the word *gohan* means both "rice" and "meal" should give you an idea of just how important the grains are in Japan. For many Japanese people, even in modern Japan where noodles and bread abound, a meal without rice is almost unthinkable. A typical family might sit down for breakfast or dinner in front of a few dishes to share—maybe simmered fish, soup, and pickles. Everyone, however, has his own bowl of rice, the heart of the meal. As a boy in a poor family, I sometimes had entire meals of rice. I remember one night, my mother brought home a special treat—octopus. There was enough for each of us to have just one slice. Still, I feasted that night—my octopus slice, soy sauce, and bowl after bowl after bowl of rice.

Much of Japanese food is designed to be eaten alongside rice. The intensely salty-sweet flavor of fish marinated in miso, for instance, and

pickles are balanced by the beautifully bland grains. Everything is essentially a condiment for the rice. This is especially true with sushi. Oyama-san taught me that while the seafood, with its striking array of colors, seems like the main event, it was really just an accessory for the rice, similar to soy sauce and wasabi. I didn't quite believe him until I ate the result of his careful cooking. The grains of his sushi rice were so perfectly cooked—tender and springy, slick and sticky—that it seemed as if he had prepared each one separately.

This was how he showed his respect for rice. He elevated it from humble grain to something special, from simple sustenance to what tasted like a luxury. Today, at my restaurants, I try to continue this tradition. I even have a mill so I can polish brown rice into perfect pearly white grains to my

exact, fussy specifications. (I figure if my customers pay more than $100 for sushi, then it had better be perfect.)

Home-cooked rice is a different animal. Unlike Oyama-san, your dinner guests will not point out the slightest imperfection. So you don't need your own mill, or years of practice—just a mother, grandmother, or Morimoto to teach you. In this chapter I take your hand and guide you through making perfect white rice—which takes barely more effort than cooking Uncle Ben's and will serve as the backbone for nearly every dish in this book. I'll show you how to make sticky-amazing sushi rice and then turn it into temaki rolls. And I'll introduce you to carefully mounded rice balls stuffed with salmon or plum; fried rice with eggs and vegetables and anything else in the fridge; and the transcendently delicious, deceptively simple chicken-and-egg dish called *oyako don*. Once you cook through the recipes in this chapter and see how satisfying the unassuming grain can be, you might never eat a meal without rice again.

BUY A RICE COOKER

You can absolutely make rice in a pot. But there's a reason that virtually everyone in Japan over the age of two owns an electric rice cooker, the single greatest gift Japan has given to the world, Nintendo aside. Cooking rice in a pot requires a little vigilance—you must make sure the water is always simmering very gently—while a rice cooker lets you press a button and go watch baseball on TV. Not only that, the cooker will keep your rice warm until you're ready to eat it, without the grains turning to mush. And unless you're a true expert, using a pot won't give you as predictably perfect grains as a cooker.

Ah, but which rice cooker is best? The answer depends on you. There are rice cookers that cost hundreds of dollars and seem to have hundreds of buttons and settings. Not even I have one of these! Then there are inexpensive cookers with just one button: you add rice and water, press cook, and that's it. I prefer the middle ground. Look for a cooker with features that you think you'll actually use—for example, the brown rice setting is magic for me and my wife, Keiko, because it makes the best brown rice you've ever tasted. And don't pay for features you won't use—a *congee* setting is only a blessing for big fans of rice porridge. Finally, make sure the cooking capacity meets your needs as well. If you love to cook for friends, don't buy a rice cooker that can make only four cups of cooked rice.

HAKUMAI

PERFECT WHITE RICE

Today, everyone wants quicker, faster, sooner. Yet just because you can buy instant rice and microwavable rice doesn't mean you should. One bite of my perfect white rice will show you why. Sure, you must take the extra step of rinsing the uncooked grains under water to wash away excess starch, but this leads to cooked rice with perfectly plump, springy grains that are blessedly free of mush and clumps. Please don't cheat and buy cheaper long-grain rice: short-grain rice—often labeled "sushi rice"—is essential, even though you're not necessarily making sushi. (If you are, flip to page 50.) The recipe below yields 6 cups of cooked rice, perfect for dinner for four people or one Morimoto. Adjusting the amount, though, is simple: just remember, always cook the rinsed rice with the same volume of water (for instance, 3 cups of rice requires 3 cups of water).

MAKES 6 CUPS

2¼ cups short-grain white rice ("sushi rice")

Put the rice in a large-mesh strainer set inside a large mixing bowl and add enough water to cover the rice. Use your hands to stir and agitate the rice to release the starch from the exterior of the grains. Empty the water, fill the bowl again, and repeat the process until the fresh water no longer becomes cloudy when you stir the rice.

Drain the rice in the strainer and shake well to help drain excess water. Let the rice sit in the strainer, stirring once or twice, until it's more or less dry to the touch, 15 to 30 minutes.

Transfer the rice to the rice cooker, add 2¼ cups of fresh water, and cook according to the manufacturer's directions. Gently fluff the rice with a plastic or wooden rice paddle and serve immediately or keep warm in the rice cooker.

FURIKAKE WITH SHRIMP SHELLS AND POTATO CHIPS

Every Japanese home has a shaker of *furikake* in the pantry. Typically a mixture of dried sea vegetables, dried fish, sesame seeds, and other seasonings, it adds salty-sweet flavor and a jolt of umami to whatever it touches. We keep it on hand mainly for those moments when all the food is gone but we're craving more rice—the wonderfully bland staple that needs just a little flavor boost.

My version builds on the classic combination with crunchy potato chips and incredibly tasty but often discarded shrimp shells (whenever you remove them from the crustaceans, save them in a freezer bag for this purpose!). A tablespoon or two turns plain white rice into a stimulating snack and adds extra excitement to rice balls (see Onigiri, page 37). But the fun doesn't stop there: *furikake* also makes a surprising and amazing topping for buttered popcorn.

Since potato chip brands vary in saltiness, remember to season the mixture to taste, keeping in mind that it should be salty enough for just a tablespoon or so to flavor a bowl of plain rice.

MAKES ABOUT 1 CUP

2 cups fresh or frozen shrimp shells
   (from about 1¼ pounds shrimp)
¾ cup loosely packed bonito flakes
   (*katsuobushi*)
½ cup coarsely crumbled salted potato
   chips
1 sheet nori, broken into several pieces
1 tablespoon toasted sesame seeds
1 teaspoon kosher salt, plus more to taste

Preheat the oven to 250°F. Spread the shrimp shells
in a single layer on a baking sheet and bake, tossing
occasionally, until completely dry and crumbly,
about 45 minutes. Cool completely.

One ingredient by one, grind the shrimp shells,
bonito flakes, potato chips, and nori in a small
food processor or large spice grinder until you
have a mixture of pieces that are about the size
of coarse sea salt (a little bigger or smaller is fine).
Nori is harder to process, so don't worry if the
pieces are a bit bigger than the rest. Combine
them all in a small container with the sesame
seeds and salt. Stir well and season with salt to
taste.

You can keep the *furikake* in an airtight container
in a cool dark place (not the refrigerator) for up to
10 days.

ONIGIRI

RICE BALLS

Go into any convenience store in Japan (or peek inside the lunch box of any kid or businessperson) and you'll see rows of the classic, portable, and shockingly tasty Japanese snack called onigiri, *triangular rice balls wrapped in nori seaweed and filled with delicious things like pickled plum or broiled salmon. Not only that, you'll also see some very clever packaging. At first, the triangle looks like seaweed pressed against rice—a recipe for soggy seaweed. But follow the instructions on the package—pull this tab, tug at that corner—and suddenly you realize there was a plastic barrier the whole time. Now your onigiri is wrapped in crisp seaweed! You don't apply such genius to a snack unless it is a national sensation. And onigiri is just that.*

At home, it makes a beautiful blank canvas. The filling can be anything you desire, from my favorite, Tuna Mayo (page 38), or enticing leftovers from last night's dinner. You can even roll the outsides in toasted sesame seeds, shichimi togarashi *(Japanese seven-spice powder), or* furikake *(page 34). The balls are easy to mold with your hands, but you can also use cookie cutters or even plastic* onigiri *molds, which are inexpensive and come in shapes such as stars, teddy bears, and octopuses.*

MAKES ABOUT 8

4 cups freshly made short-grain white rice (page 33)
Kosher salt
¾ cup leftover Sake Shioyaki (salt-grilled salmon, page 100),
    Hijiki (sweet simmered *hijiki* seaweed, page 158), or Tori No
    Teriyaki (chicken teriyaki, page 107), chopped if necessary,
    at room temperature
4 nori seaweed sheets (about 8½ by 7½ inches), halved
    lengthwise

Let the rice cool slightly, so you can handle it without burning your fingers.

Pour some salt in a small bowl. To make each ball, wet your hands slightly with water, dip two fingertips in the salt, and briefly rub your hands together to distribute the salt. Grab a ½-cup clump of rice and spread it slightly in your palm to form a ¾-inch layer.

Make a slight indentation in the center and add about a generous tablespoon of the filling, pressing lightly to flatten it if necessary. Fold the rice around the filling to enclose it completely, using a little more rice if necessary. Use both hands to shape the rice into a rough ball, then firmly pack it to form a rough triangle that has about 3-inch sides and is about 1 inch thick.

Repeat with the remaining rice and filling.

Just before you eat the rice triangles, wrap them in the nori. Serve right away, while the nori is still slightly crisp.

Tuna Mayo

Of all the fillings that wind up inside onigiri, *my favorite is* tuna mayo, *probably the one Japanese phrase every English speaker understands. It is almost exactly what its name suggests: canned tuna mixed with mayo. In particular, I recommend the Japanese variety called Kewpie, which has even more flavor than Hellmann's.*

MAKES ABOUT ½ CUP

One 5-ounce can solid light tuna (preferably oil-packed), drained
2 tablespoons mayonnaise, preferably Kewpie mayonnaise
Kosher salt

Combine the tuna and mayonnaise in a bowl and stir well, breaking up any chunks. Season with salt to taste.

YAKI ONIGIRI

GRILLED RICE BALLS

Onigiri, the rice balls sold from convenience stores and packed for school lunches, become a different kind of treat at the yakitori shop. As cooks rotate skewers of meat and vegetables over hot charcoal, they also throw unwrapped, unfilled onigiri on the grill, basting them with a dead simple sauce until they're smoky and crispy on the outside. They're especially tasty after a little too much sake.

MAKES ABOUT 8

Special Equipment
A gas or charcoal grill (grates lightly rubbed with vegetable
    oil), or a flameproof rack
A food-safe brush

4 cups freshly made short-grain white rice (page 33)
Kosher salt
¼ cup Japanese soy sauce
¼ cup mirin (sweet rice wine)

Let the rice cool slightly, so you can handle it without burning your fingers. Form the *onigiri* as instructed on pages 37–38, making sure to pack the triangles especially firmly. Do not wrap with nori. Let them cool completely. You can wrap them in plastic wrap and refrigerate them for up to a day.

When you're ready to eat, prepare the grill to cook over medium-high heat. (If you're using the flameproof rack, set it on a burner and turn the heat to medium.)

Stir together the soy sauce and mirin in a small bowl. Put the rice triangles on their sides directly on the grill or rack. Cook until the undersides are dry and slightly crispy with spots of brown, 3 to 4 minutes. Carefully flip them, brush the tops and sides with the soy sauce mixture, and cook, flipping and brushing every few minutes, until both sides have formed a crunchy crust and are golden brown with dark brown spots, about 8 minutes more. Serve right away.

OMURAISU

OMELET WITH KETCHUP-FRIED RICE

This dish—an omelet filled with ketchup-spiked fried rice—is one of several beloved Japanese classics that seem a bit odd to many Americans. Yet I've seen friends go from skeptic to convert with just one bite. Ketchup has become almost as common a sight in the Japanese pantry as soy sauce and, like soy sauce, it provides a blast of flavor and umami, in this case to leftover rice. Skilled home cooks can use a flick of their wrist to wrap the omelet around the rice in the skillet, but don't worry— my recipe offers an easier way.

SERVES 4

For the Ketchup-Fried Rice
½ pound boneless skinless chicken breast or
    thigh, cut into ½-inch pieces
¾ cup sliced (¼ inch) green beans
½ cup diced (¼ inch) carrot
4 tablespoons unsalted butter, cut into several
    pieces
2 tablespoons vegetable oil
1 cup very thinly sliced fresh shiitake mushroom
    caps
½ cup fresh or frozen corn kernels
½ cup finely chopped yellow onion
6 cups cooked short-grain white rice (page 33)
¾ cup ketchup
1 teaspoon kosher salt
Black pepper to taste

For the Omuraisu
8 large eggs
Kosher salt and black pepper
2 tablespoons unsalted butter, cut into 4 equal
    pieces
2 tablespoons vegetable oil

MAKE THE KETCHUP-FRIED RICE

Bring a medium pot of water to a boil. Add the chicken, cook for 1 minute, then add the green beans and carrot and cook, stirring occasionally, until the chicken is just cooked through and the vegetables are still crunchy, about 1 minute more. Drain well.

Heat the butter and oil in a large skillet over medium-high heat and add the chicken, green beans, carrot, mushrooms, corn, and onion. Cook, stirring, until the onion is translucent, about 3 minutes. Add the rice and cook, stirring often and breaking up the clumps but making sure not to smash the grains, until the rice is heated through, about 5 minutes.

Add the ketchup, salt, and pepper and cook, folding and stirring, until the rice is an even color, about 2 minutes. Transfer the rice to a bowl, cover, and keep warm.

MAKE THE OMURAISU

Make one omelet at a time. Crack 2 eggs into a bowl, add a generous pinch of salt and pepper, and lightly beat the eggs.

Combine ½ tablespoon of the butter with ½ tablespoon of the oil in a 10- to 12-inch nonstick skillet, set it over medium-high heat, and let the butter melt and froth, swirling the skillet. Add the beaten eggs and cook, gently pushing the edges in an inch or two as they set and swirling the pan to allow the still-raw egg to hit the pan, until the entire omelet is set but still glossy, 1 to 2 minutes.

Add a quarter of the rice to a plate, slide the omelet on top, and use a kitchen towel to tuck the edges of the eggs under the rice to make an omelet shape. Repeat with the remaining eggs and rice.

TAKIKOMI GOHAN

DASHI-SIMMERED RICE WITH VEGETABLES

This is one of the most elegant rice dishes I know: the flavors are mild but perfectly balanced, so nothing super sweet or salty or bold comes through, but the overall effect is incredibly rich and satisfying. The secret is to first simmer the vegetables in a blend of delicious liquids (dashi, mirin, sake) and then cook the rice in that magic broth.

In the old days, this dish was made in an okama, a pot with a wooden lid that was set over hot charcoal, and it browned at the bottom as the sugar in the mirin gently caramelized. For you and me, any pot will do. You can even use a rice cooker! In fact, high-end rice cookers even have a "takikomi gohan" button. My recipe calls for classic ingredients, but feel free to use parsnips instead of burdock root, sliced fresh or rehydrated dried shiitake mushrooms instead of the konnyaku, and extra chicken instead of fried tofu skins.

SERVES 4

1½ teaspoons vegetable oil

1½ teaspoons toasted sesame oil

¼ pound boneless chicken thigh, trimmed and cut into ¾-inch pieces

½ cup sliced (1½ by ½ by ⅛ inch) peeled carrot

½ cup sliced (1½ by ½ by ⅛ inch) store-bought *abura-age* (fried tofu skins)

¼ cup peeled sliced (1½ by ½ by ⅛ inch) burdock root (*gobo*) or parsnip

⅓ cup sliced (1 by ½ by ⅛ inch) gray *konnyaku* (Japanese "yam cake")

2¼ cups Dashi (dried fish and kelp stock, page 20) or Kombu Dashi (kelp stock, page 23)

2 tablespoons Japanese soy sauce

1 tablespoon sake (Japanese rice wine)

1 tablespoon mirin (sweet rice wine)

¾ teaspoon kosher salt

2 cups short-grain white rice ("sushi rice"), washed well and drained

Pour the oils in a small pot, add the chicken, set the pot over medium heat, and wait for the chicken to sizzle. Cook, stirring occasionally, until the chicken is no longer pink on the outside, about 2 minutes.

Add the carrot, *abura-age,* burdock, and *konnyaku* and stir well, then add the dashi, soy sauce, sake, mirin, and salt. Raise the heat to medium-high, bring the liquid to a strong simmer, and cook until the carrots are tender with a slight bite, 5 to 8 minutes. Use a spoon to skim off any white scum from the surface. Strain the liquid through a sieve into a large heatproof measuring cup, reserving the solids. If necessary, pour off any excess liquid or add enough water or extra dashi to give you 2 cups of liquid.

Combine the liquid and rice in a rice cooker or a medium pot and stir briefly. If you're using a rice cooker, use the white rice setting if there is one and press the "cook" button. If you're using a pot, cover it, set it over medium-high heat, and bring the liquid to a boil. Immediately reduce the heat to very low to maintain a bare simmer and cook, doing your best not to peek under the lid, until the rice has absorbed the liquid and is tender, about 15 minutes. If you are using a rice cooker, wait until the rice has finished cooking completely and the timer goes off.

Add the reserved chicken mixture (but don't stir just yet) and cover with the lid again. Remove from the heat and let the pot or rice cooker sit until the chicken mixture is hot and the rice is completely tender, at least 10 or up to 20 minutes. Stir gently but well, then serve right away.

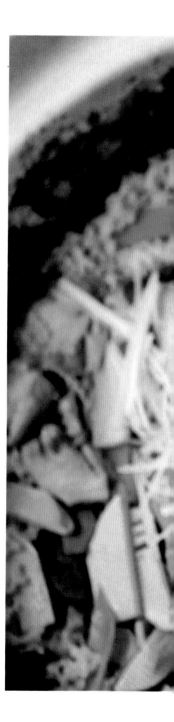

TAKIKOMI ONIGIRI

Takikomi gohan makes amazing *onigiri* (rice balls). Before you refrigerate leftovers, form them into balls as instructed on page 37. Wrap in plastic and chill for up to two days. Microwave until just warm through, then remove the plastic wrap and eat right away.

CHAHAN

JAPANESE-STYLE FRIED RICE

There is no better use for leftover rice than chahan. *A brief trip in a pan resurrects the grains and a few pantry ingredients—little more than eggs, oil, and salt—transform tired rice into a super-satisfying meal. To give the humble dish a little flair, I whip up a saucy broth filled with vegetables and shrimp and pour it on at the last minute. Of course, you can add any ingredients you like—peas or asparagus, kimchi or Japanese pickles, pork, or even, as I do at Morimoto Napa, duck confit.*

SERVES 4

¼ cup diced (¼-inch cubes) carrot
12 medium shrimp (about 6 ounces), peeled and deveined, cut
    crosswise into thirds
¼ cup fresh or frozen corn kernels
¼ cup fresh or frozen shelled edamame
¼ cup diced (¼-inch pieces) fresh shiitake mushrooms or
    rehydrated dried shiitakes (page 254)
2¼ cups low-sodium chicken stock
3 tablespoons Japanese soy sauce
3 tablespoons sake (Japanese rice wine)
2 teaspoons granulated sugar
1½ teaspoons kosher salt
3 tablespoons cornstarch
2 teaspoons toasted sesame oil
White or black pepper to taste
¼ cup vegetable oil
4 large eggs, lightly beaten
6 packed cups cooked short-grain white rice (page 33), preferably
    1 or 2 days old
1 generous tablespoon thinly sliced scallion greens

Bring a small pot of water to a boil. Add the carrot and cook 2 minutes. Add the shrimp and cook until they're just cooked through, 1 to 2 minutes more. Drain and then return them to the pot. Add the corn, edamame, shiitakes, chicken stock, soy sauce, sake, sugar, and ½ teaspoon of salt. Set the pot over medium-high heat and bring to a boil. In a small container, stir together the cornstarch and 3 tablespoons of water until smooth. Gradually

add the cornstarch mixture to the pot, stirring constantly. Let the stock mixture come to a boil again and cook just until slightly thickened, about 3 minutes. Take the pot off the heat and stir in the sesame oil and pepper to taste; keep warm, covered.

Heat the vegetable oil in a large skillet over medium-high heat until it shimmers. Add the eggs and cook, stirring constantly, until they're barely cooked, about 30 seconds. Add the rice and cook, stirring often and breaking up the clumps but making sure not to smash the grains, until the rice is heated through and the egg has browned slightly, about 4 minutes. Season with about 1 teaspoon of the salt and pepper to taste.

Divide the fried rice among 4 small bowls and firmly press down on the rice to pack it into the bowls. Overturn the bowls onto 4 large shallow bowls. Remove the bowls to reveal the mounds of rice and pour the sauce over each one. Top with the scallions and serve.

SU MESHI

SUSHI RICE

No matter how closely associated the two have become, the word sushi *doesn't mean raw fish. Sushi is the result of two words—*su, *meaning "vinegar," and* meshi, *meaning "rice"—getting smushed together. And as all real sushi chefs know, good vinegared rice is more important to top-quality sushi than even the most expensive tuna belly. That's why chefs spend years learning to cook rice to the perfect texture and to add just the right balance of sweet and tart flavors.*

Perfect sushi rice topped with pristine seafood is why customers spend hundreds of dollars to eat in near silence at the sushi temples of Tokyo. Yet sushi doesn't always have to be such a serious experience. Perfection, after all, is the enemy of fun. So here I do what home cooks all over Japan do. I let go of the methods of masters—sourcing the finest raw rice, polishing it myself, fanning the cooked grains in a giant wooden tub to eliminate moisture—to make effortless sushi rice that tastes like a master made it.

The ambitious among you will surely have fun meticulously slicing tuna and yellowtail to make nigiri sushi, *the fish-topped fingers of rice sold at sushi bars, but I recommend a less elaborate route. Make sushi rice into the rolls called* temaki *(page 53), or use it as the base for Tekka Don No Poke (Hawaiian poke-style tuna rice bowl, page 73).*

MAKES ABOUT 8 CUPS

For the Sushi Vinegar
One 2-inch square piece of kombu (dried kelp)
1 cup unseasoned rice vinegar
½ cup granulated sugar
¼ cup kosher salt

For the Rice
3 cups short-grain white rice ("sushi rice")

MORIMOTO MAGIC TRICK
TO DISTRIBUTE THE VINEGAR EVENLY, I LIKE TO HOLD A WOODEN SPATULA PARALLEL TO THE RICE AND POUR THE SUSHI VINEGAR ONTO IT AS I WAVE THE SPATULA BACK AND FORTH.

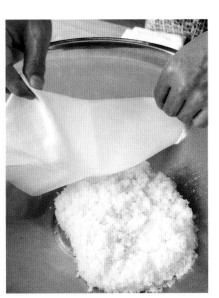

MAKE THE SUSHI VINEGAR

Briefly and gently wipe the kombu with a damp towel to remove any dirt or grit, but do not scrub off the white stuff, which is full of umami.

Combine the vinegar, sugar, salt, and kombu in a small pot and set it over medium-high heat. Cook, stirring often, just until the sugar has dissolved, about 1 minute. Do not let it boil. Let the mixture cool to room temperature.

Measure ½ cup of the vinegar mixture and set it aside. Store the rest, including the kombu, in an airtight container in the fridge for up to several months.

COOK THE RICE

Put the rice in a large mixing bowl and add enough water to cover the rice by 1 inch. Use your hands to stir and agitate the rice to release the starch from the exterior of the grains. Empty the water, fill the bowl again, and repeat the process until the fresh water no longer becomes cloudy when you stir the rice. Drain the rice in a mesh strainer, shaking well to help drain excess water. Let the rice sit in the strainer, stirring once or twice, until it's more or less dry to the touch, 15 to 30 minutes.

Combine the rice and 3 cups of fresh water in a rice cooker and cook according to the manufacturer's instructions.

While the rice is hot, gently scoop it into a bowl. Sprinkle the reserved ½ cup of sushi vinegar over the rice. Gently fold the rice to make sure the vinegar is well distributed without smashing the grains. Cover with a clean kitchen towel pressed to the surface of the rice and let the rice cool to just slightly above room temperature before using for *temaki* (hand rolls, page 53).

CHIRASHI ZUSHI
SCATTERED SUSHI

Every good sushi restaurant offers a rendition of this wide bowl of vinegared rice "scattered" (*chirashi*) with colorful toppings. At the best *sushi-ya,* this is an assortment of the finest seafood, often raw and meticulously sliced. At home, the toppings can be virtually anything. *Tamagoyaki* (Japanese omelet, page 115), poached shrimp, creamy slices of avocado, crunchy julienned cucumber, salmon roe—it's up to you!

TEMAKI: HAND ROLLS

To this day, my favorite kind of sushi to serve is temaki, *nori rolled by hand into a cylinder or cone shape around vinegared rice and a filling. It's the only type of sushi—perhaps the only dish of any kind, in fact—that the chef hands directly to the diner. When else does a chef get to ignore the plate entirely? There's a reason, of course: passing it directly to the customer is meant to encourage her to eat it immediately, so the nori is super-crispy and crackles under her teeth as she bites.*

This serve-it-right-away commandment makes temaki *perfect for a DIY sushi party. Set out a stack of nori, a big bowl of rice, and various fillings—traditional combos like* ume-shiso *(a tart pickled plum and Japanese mint-like herb) or modern ones like spicy tuna and tuna mayo (page 38). You can play sushi chef for the first few rolls, showing them how it's done and reminding them to bite into the roll right away, then let your guests construct their own. Oh, did I mention there's no bamboo mat required?*

Remember, the recipes I include here are just ideas—the fun is playing around with combinations yourself.

Spicy Tuna Temaki

MAKES 8 HAND ROLLS

2 tablespoons mayonnaise
1 teaspoon *tobanjan* (chile bean sauce), preferably a Japanese brand
½ teaspoon toasted sesame oil
½ teaspoon freshly squeezed lemon juice
½ teaspoon freshly squeezed lime juice
4 nori seaweed sheets (about 8½ by 7½ inches), halved lengthwise
About 2 cups cooked, vinegared short-grain white rice (page 50), at
    room temperature
½ pound sushi-grade tuna, cut into approximately 3 by ½ by
    ½-inch pieces
Heaping ¼ cup thinly sliced scallion greens

Combine the mayonnaise, *tobanjan,* sesame oil, lemon juice, and lime
juice in a small bowl and stir well. It keeps covered in the fridge for up to
2 days.

To make each hand roll, hold a piece of nori shiny side down in an open
palm. Lightly moisten your other hand with water and grab about a ¼-cup
clump of rice, compress it slightly to form a rough oval, and add it to one

of the short sides of the nori, about 1 inch from the edge. Firmly press the rice with your pointer finger to make a lengthwise divot in the center. To the divot, add about 1 teaspoon of the mayo, 2 pieces of the tuna, and about 2 teaspoons of the scallions.

Roll the nori around the filling to form a cone or cylinder. Eat right away.

Ume-Shiso Temaki

MAKES 8 HAND ROLLS

4 nori seaweed sheets (about 8½ by 7½ inches), halved
  lengthwise
About 2 cups cooked, vinegared short-grain white rice
  (page 50), at room temperature
5 *umeboshi* (Japanese pickled "plums"), pitted, roughly chopped,
  and smushed to a paste
8 fresh shiso leaves (also called Japanese mint and perilla)
¼ pound crunchy cucumber (preferably Japanese, English, or
  Persian), peeled, seeded, and cut into thin matchsticks

To make each hand roll, hold a piece of nori shiny side down in an open palm. Lightly moisten your other hand with water and grab about a ¼-cup clump of rice, compress it slightly to form a rough oval, and add it to one of the short sides of the nori, about 1 inch from the edge. Firmly press the rice with your pointer finger to make a lengthwise divot in the center. Spread about ¼ teaspoon of the *umeboshi* in the divot, top with a shiso leaf, and a generous pinch of the cucumber.

Roll the nori around the filling to form a cone or cylinder. Eat right away.

Vegetable Temaki

MAKES 8 HAND ROLLS

4 nori seaweed sheets (about 8½ by 7½ inches), halved lengthwise

About 2 cups cooked, vinegared short-grain white rice (page 50), at room temperature

About 1½ teaspoons wasabi paste

About 1½ tablespoons *furikake,* store-bought or homemade (page 34)

8 fresh shiso leaves (also called Japanese mint and perilla)

¼ pound crunchy cucumber (preferably Japanese, English, or Persian), seeded and cut into 4 by ¼-inch matchsticks

2 ounces carrot (about ½ of a medium carrot), peeled and cut into 4 by ¼-inch matchsticks

1 loosely packed cup *kaiware daikon* (radish sprouts) or another microgreen (optional)

To make each hand roll, hold a piece of nori shiny side down in an open palm. Lightly moisten your other hand with water and grab about a ¼-cup clump of rice, compress it slightly to form a rough oval, and add it to one of the short sides of the nori, about 1 inch from the edge. Firmly press

the rice with your pointer finger to make a lengthwise divot in the center. Spread on a little wasabi and add a generous sprinkle of *furikake*, 1 shiso leaf, 1 piece of cucumber, 1 piece of carrot, and a generous pinch of *kaiware daikon*.

Roll the nori around the filling to form a cone or cylinder. Eat right away.

California Temaki

MAKES 8 HAND ROLLS

½ firm-ripe Hass avocado
4 nori seaweed sheets (about 8½ by 7½ inches), halved lengthwise
About 2 cups cooked, vinegared short-grain white rice (page 50), at
    room temperature
¼ pound crunchy cucumber (preferably Japanese, English, or
    Persian), peeled, seeded, and cut into thin matchsticks
¼ pound *surimi* (mock crab) or fresh lump crabmeat
2 ounces *tobiko* (flying-fish roe; optional)

Remove the pit of the avocado, and peel off the skin as if you're peeling an egg. Cut into long, approximately ¼-inch-thick slices.

To make each hand roll, hold a piece of nori shiny side down in an open palm. Lightly moisten your other hand with water and grab about a ¼-cup clump of rice, compress it slightly to form a rough oval, and add it to one of the short sides of the nori, about 1 inch from the edge. Firmly press the rice with your pointer finger to make a lengthwise divot in the center.

To each, add a slice of avocado, a generous pinch of the cucumber, a pointer-finger-size piece of *surimi* or generous tablespoon of crabmeat, and 1 generous teaspoon of *tobiko*.

Roll the nori around the filling to form a cone or cylinder. Eat right away.

JAPANESE GRANDMOTHER WISDOM

Salt is like fairy dust. It can make amazing things happen. Before you slice the cucumbers, lightly sprinkle kosher salt onto them and roughly rub the salt against the skin. This technique, known as *itazuri,* dislodges an invisible, slightly bitter substance from the skin. Briefly rinse it off, dry the cucumber, and proceed with the recipe.

BATTERA

PRESSED MACKEREL SUSHI

Even though battera's popularity in Japan surpasses that of the spicy tuna roll, few Americans have ever heard of this tasty type of sushi: mackerel cured to preserve its freshness and mellow its fishiness, leaving a fresh sea flavor accented by vinegar. Once a specialty of Kansai, an inland region that centuries ago lacked access to fresh fish, battera offers a window into a time long before tuna could travel from Tokyo to New York in a day.

SERVES 6 TO 8

Special Equipment
Bamboo sushi mat (*makisu*)

Two 6- to 7-ounce Atlantic mackerel (*saba*) fillets
½ cup fine salt
About 2 cups unseasoned rice vinegar
4 thin lemon slices
6 fresh shiso leaves (also called Japanese mint and perilla)
2 tablespoons julienned pickled ginger (*gari*)
2 cups cooked, vinegared short-grain white rice (page 50)

At least 2½ hours and up to 5½ hours before you plan to eat, put the fillets on a plate and generously sprinkle the salt onto both sides. Gently shake to remove any excess, transfer the fillets to a cake rack set over a large plate, and let them sit at room temperature for 1½ hours.

Rinse the fillets under running water, rubbing them gently, then pat dry and transfer to two resealable bags. Divide the vinegar and lemon slices between the bags, and refrigerate for 45 minutes. Drain the fillets and pat them dry again.

Put the fillets skin side up on a cutting board. Starting at an edge of the widest end of each fillet, pinch the transparent top layer of skin, gently pull it away from the shiny skin, and discard it.

(Recipe continues on page 64)

(Continued from page 61)

Put the fillet skin side down on a square of plastic wrap. Use tweezers or needle-nose pliers to remove the pin bones: identify the bones by running a finger along the center of the fillet. One by one, grab them at the tip with the tweezers or pliers and firmly pull at an angle to remove them. Feel for any additional bones or cartilage, especially near the belly, and remove.

Working one at a time, butterfly the fillets: Arrange the fillet perpendicular to your cutting board. Identify the center of the fillet, where the spine used to be; you are going to butterfly the fish on both sides of the spine. Hold your knife parallel to the cutting board with the blade aligned with the spine. Cut through the flesh of the fish, stopping about ½ inch before reaching the edge. Use your fingers to open the cut flesh like a book. Repeat on the other side of the spine. Then repeat with the other fillet.

Put the fillet skin side down on a square of plastic wrap. Arrange the shiso leaves in a single layer along the center of each fillet. Evenly spread the ginger onto the shiso leaves. Evenly spread the rice in a 2-inch-wide stripe along the center of the fillet. Wrap each in the plastic wrap to form a tight log. Put the sushi mat on the cutting board so the slats run right to left. One at a time, transfer the plastic-wrapped logs to the mat, fold one edge of the mat over the log, and use your hands to press firmly on the top and sides to compress the *battera* slightly.

Let the plastic-wrapped log rest at room temperature for at least 15 minutes or up to 3 hours. The longer it rests, the more flavor the sushi rice will absorb from the fish, shiso, and ginger. When you're ready to eat, remove the plastic wrap, cut crosswise into ¾-inch-thick slices, and serve.

DONBURI
Rice bowls

Donburi, or *don* for short, encompasses a wide range of dishes that take a similar form: a large bowl filled with rice, then topped with flavor-packed ingredients cooked in an irresistible sauce. Rice bowls like this might seem simple and old-fashioned, but they're actually a fairly modern concept in Japan. While rice has a long history on the Japanese table, it was traditionally served plain and in its own bowl. It wasn't until a few centuries ago, when the population became busy and needed faster meal options, that these one-bowl meals took hold. Today, they're everywhere in Japan, at fast-food-style rice bowl restaurants and in homes around the country.

OYAKO DON

CHICKEN AND EGG RICE BOWL

This rice bowl is elegantly simple—so simple that you might flip past this page without giving it a second thought. Do not make this mistake! Oyako means "parent and child" and refers poetically to the rice bowl's star ingredients, chicken and egg. The pairing might not sound exciting, but I assure you that once they're simmered in a magical mixture of dashi, soy sauce, and mirin, they transform into an incredibly satisfying dish that's so much more than the sum of its parts.

People often cook this dish in a special oyako don *pan, but you'll have great success in a small skillet. Just don't try to double or quadruple the amounts in a larger skillet—it won't turn out right. Instead, treat this dish as a great lunch or dinner for yourself. You deserve it!*

MAKES 1 HEARTY MEAL

⅓ cup Dashi (dried fish and kelp stock, page 20) or Kombu Dashi (kelp stock, page 23)
1 tablespoon plus 1 teaspoon Japanese soy sauce
1 tablespoon plus 1 teaspoon mirin (sweet rice wine)
¼ teaspoon granulated sugar
5 ounces boneless skinless chicken thighs, cut into about 1-inch pieces
1 teaspoon toasted sesame oil
2 large eggs, beaten
¼ cup very thinly sliced scallions (white and light green parts), preferably cut into long diagonal slices
1½ cups cooked short-grain white rice (page 33), hot
Large pinch *kizame* (shredded) nori or ¼ nori seaweed sheet, cut into thin strips with scissors

Combine the dashi, soy sauce, mirin, and sugar in a medium bowl and stir until the sugar has dissolved.

Combine the chicken and sesame oil in a small skillet, stir well, and set it over medium-high heat. Once the chicken begins to sizzle, cook, stirring occasionally, until the chicken is no longer pink on the outside, about 3 minutes.

Reduce the heat to medium, add the dashi mixture, and let it come to a simmer. In a steady stream, pour the eggs evenly over the chicken and sprinkle the scallions on top. Cover the skillet with a lid, leaving the lid slightly ajar. Reduce the heat to maintain a simmer and cook, shaking the pan occasionally to make sure the eggs don't stick to the skillet, until the eggs have just fully set, 6 to 8 minutes. There will be a little liquid left in the skillet.

Spoon the rice into a shallow serving bowl. Bring the skillet to the bowl, then tilt and wiggle the skillet to slide the contents, liquid and all, onto the rice. Top with the nori. Eat right away.

KATSU DON

PORK CUTLET AND EGG RICE BOWL

Home cooks don't fry a whole batch of tonkatsu *(breaded pork cutlets) just to make* katsu don. *No,* katsu don *is what happens when you find yourself at home with an empty stomach and a cutlet left over from the night before. Since the cutlets will no longer be crispy anyway, you give up on crispness altogether and go straight for flavor, simmering the pork in seasoned dashi and adding egg for extra richness. Then you slide the omelet-like result onto a bowl of hot rice.*

SERVES 1

⅓ cup Dashi (dried fish and kelp stock, page 20) or Kombu Dashi
   (kelp stock, page 23)
1 tablespoon plus 1 teaspoon Japanese soy sauce
1 tablespoon plus 1 teaspoon mirin (sweet rice wine)
¼ teaspoon granulated sugar
¼ cup thinly sliced white onion
1 *tonkatsu* (Japanese-style fried pork cutlet, page 215), cut crosswise
   into ¾-inch-thick slices
2 large eggs, lightly beaten
¼ cup very thinly sliced scallions or roughly chopped mitsuba
1½ cups cooked short-grain white rice (page 33), hot

Combine the dashi, soy sauce, mirin, and sugar in a small bowl and stir. Spread the onion in a small nonstick skillet, top with the slices of cutlet, and pour the dashi mixture over the cutlet. Set the skillet over medium-high heat, let it come to a simmer, and cover the skillet.

Reduce the heat to maintain a simmer and cook until the onion has wilted, about 3 minutes. Baste the cutlet with the liquid and scoop some of the onion on top of the cutlet. In a steady stream, pour the eggs evenly over the cutlet and sprinkle on the scallions or mitsuba. Cover the skillet again and cook just until the eggs have fully set, about 3 minutes. There will be a little liquid left in the skillet.

Put the rice in a large bowl. Bring the skillet to the bowl, then tilt and wiggle the skillet to slide the contents, liquid and all, onto the rice.

SUTEKI DON

STEAK RICE BOWLS WITH SPICY
TERIYAKI SAUCE

When I'm eager for beef at one of the busy Japanese lunch shops that specialize in donburi *(one-bowl meals of rice topped with a variety of simple foods), I usually order* gyu don, *thinly shaved beef and onion simmered in slightly sweet sauce. But I must say that after living in America for more than two decades, I just as often crave slices of* suteki *(that is, steak spelled phonetically, if you have a strong Japanese accent). I opt for the relatively inexpensive and super-flavorful skirt, sear it until it's charred on the outside and pink in the center, then spoon on teriyaki sauce spiked with butter and chile-bean sauce. Over rice and alongside the simple vegetable stir-fry called* yasai itame *(page 173), steak becomes a balanced meal.*

SERVES 4

1 pound skirt steak, outside fat trimmed, patted dry
Kosher salt and ground black pepper
1 tablespoon vegetable oil
1 cup teriyaki sauce (page 108)
4 tablespoons unsalted butter
1 tablespoon plus 1 teaspoon *tobanjan* (chile bean sauce), preferably
   a Japanese brand
1 teaspoon finely grated garlic
1 tablespoon cornstarch
6 cups cooked short-grain white rice (page 33), warm
¼ cup thinly sliced scallions (green parts only)
1 teaspoon toasted sesame seeds

Prepare a grill to cook over medium-high heat or preheat a large heavy skillet over high heat. Cut the steak crosswise into a few pieces if necessary to fit in the skillet. Season both sides with salt and pepper and drizzle with the oil.

Cook, flipping once, until both sides are deep brown and the steak is cooked how you like it, about 8 minutes for medium rare. Let the meat rest while you make the sauce.

Combine the teriyaki sauce, butter, *tobanjan,* and garlic in a small saucepan, set it over medium heat, and bring to a boil. Meanwhile, combine the cornstarch with 1 tablespoon water and stir until smooth. When the teriyaki mixture comes to a simmer, stir in the cornstarch mixture. Cook, stirring occasionally, just until the sauce turns shiny and thickens slightly, 3 minutes.

Divide the rice among shallow bowls and spoon about 3 tablespoons of sauce over each one. Thinly slice the steak against the grain. Top each bowl with the steak slices, spoon on the remaining sauce, and sprinkle on the scallions and sesame seeds. Serve right away.

TEKKA DON NO POKE

HAWAIIAN POKE-STYLE TUNA RICE BOWL

Once you secure sushi-grade tuna, this meal in a bowl takes almost no effort to make. I upgrade the typical tekka don—*sliced raw tuna, often briefly marinated in soy sauce—by merging it with the Hawaiian dish tuna poke (pronounced PO-kay), which I fell for while opening my restaurant in Waikiki. The cubes of luscious crimson fish dressed with a little salt, sugar, and spice taste great over wonderfully plain white rice or less traditional but no less delicious sushi rice.*

SERVES 4

¼ cup Japanese soy sauce

1 tablespoon plus 1 teaspoon mirin (sweet rice wine)

2 teaspoons toasted sesame oil

1 to 2 teaspoons *tobanjan* (chile bean sauce), preferably a
    Japanese brand

1 teaspoon granulated sugar

1 pound sushi-grade tuna, cut into ½-inch cubes

½ medium Hass avocado, peeled, pitted, cut into ½-inch
    pieces

6 cups cooked short-grain white rice (page 33) or cooked,
    vinegared short-grain white rice (page 50), warm

1 nori seaweed sheet

¼ cup thinly sliced fresh shiso leaves (also called Japanese
    mint and perilla) or scallion greens

1 teaspoon toasted sesame seeds

Combine the soy sauce, mirin, sesame oil, *tobanjan,* and sugar in a medium mixing bowl and stir until the sugar dissolves. Add the tuna and avocado to the bowl, toss well, and set aside to marinate for a few minutes but no more than 5 minutes.

Divide the rice among 4 wide bowls. Top each bowl with the tuna and avocado, leaving the sauce behind. Then drizzle the sauce over the tuna and avocado. Tear the nori into small pieces and scatter some over each bowl; top with the shiso and sesame seeds. Eat right away.

SUPU

Soups スープ

The importance of soup is sometimes difficult for my Western friends to wrap their heads around. For them, soup is a once-in-a-while dish, maybe an appetizer at a restaurant or, on a winter's night, the meal itself along with bread. Not for Japanese people. We eat it every day. We eat it for dinner, lunch, and breakfast—believe me, miso soup with rice and pickles beats eggs on toast any day. No truly balanced Japanese meal is complete without it. Light and nourishing, soup provides contrast to the starchy rice, intensely sweet and salty stewed fish, and other dishes on the table.

In this chapter, you'll find some of my favorites. There's the classic miso soup, of course, and I can't wait for you to try it again—for the first time. You see, it's different when it's made with care. And two variations await you, one made with briny clams and intriguing red miso and another that's especially hearty, chock-full of root vegetables and pork belly. Not only that—there's the revelatory Japanese take on Chinese egg drop, a countryside version that one-ups chicken noodle and a luxurious broth that celebrates the aroma of mushrooms.

MISO SHIRU

MISO SOUP WITH TOFU

You know those little packets of dehydrated miso soup with tiny cubes of dried tofu? They need to be gathered up and sent into space—they're fit for astronaut food and nothing else. The real thing is unbelievably delicious, made with barely more than dashi stock and high-quality, umami-filled miso. Once dashi becomes one of your kitchen staples, the soup comes together nearly as fast as the instant version and tastes a hundred times as good. It's so easy that you might even start serving it for breakfast, as many Japanese cooks do, along with rice and pickles.

The key to making the soup is not cooking the miso too much, which destroys its delicate flavor and healthful properties. Be careful, then, not to let the broth come to a boil or cook for more than a minute or two after adding the miso.

SERVES 4

4 cups Dashi (dried fish and kelp stock, page 20) or Kombu
   Dashi (kelp stock, page 23)
¼ cup *shiro* (white) miso, plus more if necessary
½ cup drained silken tofu
1 generous tablespoon thinly sliced scallion (preferably light
   green parts)
2 tablespoons dried wakame seaweed, soaked in cold water for
   5 minutes, then drained well

Bring the dashi to a very gentle simmer in a small pot. Put the miso in a small bowl, spoon in about ½ cup of the hot dashi, and stir, breaking up clumps, until very smooth. Pour the mixture back into the pot.

Use a spoon to scoop small chunks of the tofu into the pot. Add the scallion and seaweed, stir very gently, and wait just until the tofu is heated through, about 1 minute. Season with more miso to taste (mixing it with a little hot soup before adding it). Ladle the soup into bowls and eat right away.

ASARI NO MISO SHIRU

MISO SOUP WITH CLAMS

The standard miso soup is subtle and soothing. This version is bolder, alive with the briny flavor of clams and particularly complex if you choose to use aka (red) miso, a darker, caramel-y cousin of the more common white miso. The Japanese man in me craves a big bowl of rice to eat alongside, but now that I've lived in the United States for more than two decades, I wouldn't refuse crusty bread to sop up the irresistible broth.

SERVES 4

Special Equipment
Cheesecloth

4 cups Dashi (dried fish and kelp stock, page 20) or Kombu
    Dashi (kelp stock, page 23)
¼ cup sake (Japanese rice wine)
24 Manila or littleneck clams, scrubbed well and rinsed (see Note)
¼ cup *shiro* (white) or *aka* (red) miso
1 tablespoon thinly sliced scallion

Combine the dashi, sake, and clams in a medium pot, set over medium-high heat, and bring to a simmer. Adjust the heat to maintain a gentle simmer and cook, stirring occasionally once the clams begin to open, until they've all opened, about 3 minutes. Turn off the heat.

Transfer the clams to a small bowl. To remove any lingering sand from the clams, strain the broth through a sieve lined with two layers of cheesecloth or a sturdy paper towel into a new small pot. Bring the broth to a very gentle simmer over low heat.

Put the miso in a small bowl, spoon in about ½ cup of the broth, and stir, breaking up clumps, until very smooth. Pour the mixture back into the pot. Add the clams to the pot and cook until they're warmed through, about 30 seconds. Turn off the heat, sprinkle on the scallion, and serve immediately.

Note: Sometimes clams have sand in their shells. To remove the sand and spare yourself a gritty soup, fill a medium pot with water and add enough salt so the water tastes as salty as the sea. Add the clams and refrigerate for at least 4 hours or up to 12 hours. Drain and rinse the clams well before you make the soup.

TONJIRU

HEARTY MISO SOUP WITH PORK AND VEGETABLES

Many Americans have fond memories of chili bubbling away on the stove on a cold winter day. The closest equivalent for me is this hearty rendition of miso soup, so substantial that miso stew seems like a more appropriate description. Easy to prepare and brimming with healthy ingredients, tonjiru *is the kind of dish busy families eat for weeknight suppers. I like to use an array of root vegetables from the farmers' market—earthy-sweet sunchokes, striking golden beets, which won't stain the soup like red ones—but the combination is up to you and the soup will satisfy even if you have only carrots and potatoes.*

SERVES 4 TO 6

3 tablespoons toasted sesame oil

½ pound pork belly, cut into thin, bite-size slices

1 cup roughly chopped (into irregular ½-inch pieces) gray *konnyaku* (Japanese "yam cake")

1 cup roughly chopped (into irregular ¾-inch pieces) peeled carrot

1 cup roughly chopped (into irregular ½-inch pieces) peeled burdock (*gobo*) or parsnip

1 cup roughly chopped (into irregular ¾-inch pieces) peeled golden beets

1 cup roughly chopped (into irregular ¾-inch pieces) peeled sunchokes or daikon radish

6 medium fresh or rehydrated (page 254) dried shiitake mushroom caps, quartered

10 cups Dashi (dried fish and kelp stock, page 20) or Kombu Dashi (kelp stock, page 23)

⅔ cup *shiro* (white) miso

1 teaspoon finely grated peeled ginger

½ cup very thinly sliced scallions (white and light green parts only)

Japanese chile powder (*ichimi*) to taste

Combine the oil and pork in a large pot and set the pot over medium heat. Cook, stirring occasionally, until the pork is no longer pink, about 3 minutes. Add the *konnyaku,* carrot, burdock, beets, sunchokes, mushrooms, and dashi. Increase the heat to bring the dashi to a boil, then reduce the heat to maintain a gentle simmer. Skim off any froth from the surface.

Stir in about half of the miso and cook at a simmer until the beets are tender with a slight bite, 20 to 25 minutes. Put the remaining miso in a small bowl, spoon in some of the hot dashi mixture, and stir, breaking up clumps, until very smooth. Stir the mixture into the pot. Reduce the heat to low, cook for 5 minutes more, and turn off the heat.

Stir in the ginger, ladle the soup into bowls, and top each bowl with scallions and chile powder.

JAPANESE GRANDMOTHER WISDOM

Sure, you could use a knife to cut the *konnyaku* into pieces, but many grandmothers use their hands to break it into regular pieces. Not only is this easier, but the rough crannies this method creates actually help the pieces absorb the flavor of the broth.

TAMAGO SUPU

JAPANESE EGG DROP SOUP

You've probably ordered egg drop soup from a Chinese restaurant and admired the wispy streaks of egg in the rich chicken broth. A great example of Chinese influence on Japanese cuisine, this soup is even lighter thanks to dashi stock but still packed with flavor, with those same delicate strands of egg suspended in the broth. It makes the perfect last-minute addition to a meal: if you have dashi on hand— which I hope I've convinced you that you always should—the dish is practically already made.

SERVES 4

6 cups Dashi (dried fish and kelp stock, page 20), Kombu Dashi
   (kelp stock, page 23), or low-sodium chicken stock
½ pound silken tofu, drained and cut into ½-inch cubes
¼ cup *usukuchi* (Japanese light-colored soy sauce)
2 tablespoons dried wakame seaweed, soaked in water for
   5 minutes and drained well
1 tablespoon plus 1 teaspoon sake (Japanese rice wine)
1½ teaspoons kosher salt
3 tablespoons cornstarch
4 large eggs, lightly beaten
1 tablespoon plus 1 teaspoon toasted sesame oil
¼ cup very thinly sliced scallions (white and light green parts)

Combine the dashi, tofu, *usukuchi,* seaweed, sake, and salt in a medium pot. Bring the dashi mixture to a simmer over medium-high heat. Meanwhile, combine the cornstarch with 3 tablespoons water in a small bowl and stir until smooth. When the dashi comes to a simmer, stir in the cornstarch mixture and let simmer for 2 minutes.

Drizzle the eggs into the soup in a circular motion, stir gently but well, and continue to cook for about 30 seconds. Divide among 4 bowls, then drizzle on the sesame oil and sprinkle on the scallions.

DANGO JIRU

JAPANESE-STYLE CHICKEN
AND DUMPLING SOUP

This is the Japanese equivalent of Jewish penicillin, also known as chicken noodle soup. It's quintessential grandmother cooking at its best. Instead of chicken broth, we use smoky dashi, and instead of noodles, we make cool, craggy gnocchi-like dumplings out of just flour and water. Every family throughout the countryside has its own version. This is my favorite.

SERVES 4

1 tablespoon vegetable oil
Generous ¼ pound boneless skinless chicken thighs (about
    2 small thighs), cut into 1-inch pieces
1 cup thick batons (about 1 by ½ inch) peeled, seeded kabocha
    or another winter squash
¾ cup chopped (about ¼-inch-thick bite-size pieces) peeled
    daikon
½ cup matchsticks peeled burdock (*gobo*) or parsnip
½ cup matchsticks peeled carrot
4 medium fresh or rehydrated (page 254) dried shiitake
    mushroom caps, quartered
5 cups Dashi (dried fish and kelp stock, page 20) or Kombu
    Dashi (kelp stock, page 23)
2 tablespoons sake (Japanese rice wine)
1 tablespoon *usukuchi* (Japanese light-colored soy sauce)
2 teaspoons kosher salt
¾ cup cake flour or all-purpose flour

Combine the oil and chicken in a medium pot and set the pot over medium heat. Cook, stirring occasionally, until the chicken is no longer pink, 3 to 4 minutes. Add the vegetables and cook, stirring occasionally, for 2 minutes. Add the dashi and increase the heat to bring the dashi to a boil. Skim off any froth from the surface. Reduce the heat to maintain a gentle simmer and cook until the vegetables are tender with a slight bite, about 10 minutes. Stir in the sake, *usukuchi,* and salt.

Increase the heat to bring the liquid to a strong simmer. In a small bowl, whisk together the cake flour and ¼ cup plus 2 tablespoons water until very smooth. Add the mixture by the soup spoonful into the broth, leaving some space between each addition. The mixture will sink to the bottom. Do not stir. After about 4 minutes the dumplings will begin to rise from the bottom. Continue to cook until the dumplings are no longer gummy in the center, about 6 minutes more. Serve immediately.

JAPANESE GRANDMOTHER WISDOM

Unlike thin carrot or potato skins, the peel you remove from the outside of daikon before simmering the flesh is thicker, so there will be plenty of trimmings once you've prepared it for this soup. But don't throw away those daikon peels! For the cause of frugality and deliciousness, grandmothers reserve them, slice them, and use the crisp slivers to make *kinpira* (page 171).

DOBIN MUSHI

AROMATIC "TEA POT" SOUP WITH
MUSHROOMS, FISH, AND SHRIMP

When someone orders dobin mushi *at one of my restaurants, I like to peek out from the kitchen and watch as the dish arrives at the table. With a flourish, the waiter sets down an earthenware teapot and cup on a wooden plank. At first, customers look perplexed, probably thinking, "Hey, I thought I ordered soup!" Then I watch confusion turn to rapture as the waiter pours the broth into the cup and everyone breathes in its incredible aroma.*

This perfume comes from matsutake, *the prized pine mushroom that arrives in autumn and fetches up to $1,000 per pound. The teapot, called a* dobin, *doesn't just contribute a level of ceremony but also serves as the cooking vessel and locks in the aroma until it's time to eat. My version makes a few small concessions. Fragrant chanterelle mushrooms stand in for impractical* matsutake, *roasted chestnuts take the place of the classic gingko, and lime makes a suitable substitute for the hard-to-find Japanese citrus* sudachi, *which is squeezed over the broth at the last minute. If you must, but only if you must, you can make this dish in one pot and not individual* dobin. *Just be sure the pot is attractive enough to bring to the table and be sure to remove the lid with your guests gathered round.*

SERVES 4

Special Equipment
4 small *dobin* teapots (highly recommended)

3 ounces golden chanterelle mushrooms
4 cups Dashi (dried fish and kelp stock, page 20) or Kombu
   Dashi (kelp stock, page 23)
4 teaspoons *usukuchi* (Japanese light-colored soy sauce)
4 teaspoons sake (Japanese rice wine)
1 teaspoon kosher salt
8 thin, bite-size slices boneless skinless chicken thigh (from
   1 small thigh)

(Ingredients continue on the next page)

1½ ounces delicate white-fleshed fish fillets (such as flounder, red snapper, or sea bass), cut into 8 thin bite-size slices

4 medium shrimp, peeled and deveined, halved crosswise

8 drained canned gingko nuts or 4 jarred or vacuum-packed roasted chestnuts, halved

¼ cup loosely packed very roughly chopped mitsuba or flat-leaf parsley

4 very small lime wedges

PREPARE THE DISH

Briefly rinse the mushrooms under cold running water to remove any grit and pat dry. Trim the very bottom of the stems and cut the mushrooms through the stem into ¼-inch-thick slices.

Combine the dashi, soy sauce, sake, and salt in a small pot and bring to a simmer over medium-high heat. Meanwhile, divide the chicken, fish, shrimp, mushrooms, and chestnuts among the teapots. Set a small rack in a large, wide pot that can accommodate all 4 *dobin* (or 2 large pots to split up the *dobin*) and add ½ inch of water to the pot. If you do not have a rack that fits into your pots, you can invert ramekins to serve as pedestals for the *dobin*. Bring the water in the pot to a boil over medium-high heat. Pour the hot dashi mixture over the chicken mixture, cover the *dobin,* and place them into the prepared pot. Cover the pot with a lid or with a double layer of foil and steam until the chicken is fully cooked, about 5 minutes. Try not to lift the lid often.

SERVE THE DISH

Add the mitsuba or parsley, re-cover, turn off the heat, and let the mixture steep for 1 minute. Bring the pot or pots to the table and lift the lid in front of your guests so they can smell the wonderful aroma that's released. Divide the broth among 4 small bowls, then spoon out the mushrooms and other ingredients. Serve right away with the lime wedges for squeezing over each portion.

YAKU 焼く

To grill, broil, and sear

Japanese cooks do things differently. We tend not to brown meat in a screaming hot skillet, like the French. We don't cook with woks over roaring flames, like the Chinese. Still, our high-heat cooking—grilling, searing, and roasting—thrills like no other. I may be biased, but nowhere is grilling as simple and as tremendously tasty as it is in Japanese cuisine. The secret? Our knack for umami—generated by soy sauce, miso, and rice vinegar, among others—which incidentally is exactly why Americans love barbecue sauce and ketchup so much. In fact, our dishes have so much flavor power that stovetop cooking and broiling deliver as well.

A YAKITORI PARTY

GRILLED CHICKEN AND VEGETABLE SKEWERS

In Japan yakitori is restaurant food, and there are few places I'd rather be than a yakitori-ya, *sitting elbow to elbow with fellow diners and emptying skewer after skewer of chicken meatballs, beef tongue, and shishito peppers. In America, where everyone with a backyard seems to have a gleaming grill, these grilled skewers are a home cook's dream—simple to make for weeknight dinner and easy to scale up for a party.*

Though virtually any ingredients that can be impaled are fair game, my recipe focuses on chicken. Yakitori literally means "grilled chicken," and many restaurants offer every part imaginable, from tail to tendon. Here I stick to the most flavorful parts a home cook can get, and present them tare-style *(glazed with sauce), rather than the more minimalist* shio-style *(with just salt). Yet* shio *style is fantastic as well, especially when served with Japanese seven-spice powder and yuzu kosho (an intense condiment made from chile and citrus rind that's available at most Japanese markets and online).*

SERVES 6

Special Equipment
A grill (preferably charcoal)
42 bamboo skewers, soaked in water for 30 minutes
A food-safe brush

Twelve ¾-inch-thick half-moon slices Japanese sweet potato
2 tablespoons vegetable oil, plus more for the grill grates
12 chicken wingettes
Kosher salt
24 large shishito peppers
¾ pound boneless chicken thighs, cut into 1-inch pieces
1 bunch scallions, white and light green parts, cut into 1½-inch
    lengths
¾ pound chicken livers, trimmed of white pockets and cut into
    1-inch pieces
Chicken meatballs (page 98)
About 1 cup teriyaki sauce (page 108)
Shichimi togarashi (Japanese seven-spice powder) to taste

Up to one day in advance, put the sweet potato in a small pot, add enough water to cover, and bring to a simmer over medium-high heat. Reduce the heat and cook just until fully tender, about 8 minutes.

Prepare the grill to cook over medium-high heat and lightly rub the grill grates with vegetable oil.

Leave the wingettes unskewered for now. Season the wingettes lightly with salt and grill, skin side down and covered, until fully cooked and slightly crispy, about 15 minutes. Let them cool to the touch.

Meanwhile, toss the sweet potato and shishitos with the oil and ½ teaspoon salt. Skewer the sweet potato slices lengthwise; skewer the chicken thigh and scallions so they alternate on the skewer; skewer the liver, leaving about ¼ inch of space between each piece; use two parallel skewers to skewer the shishito peppers (4 peppers per pair of skewers) and the wingettes (2 wingettes per pair of skewers); skewer the meatballs (see Note).

Reserve the wingettes on a baking sheet. Season the chicken thigh and liver lightly with salt. Grill (it's best if the exposed skewers aren't directly over the flame), turning over once, just until light golden and fully cooked, 5 to 8 minutes.

Transfer the skewers to the baking sheet with the wingettes. Generously brush the chicken thigh, liver, wingettes, and meatballs all over with teriyaki sauce. Grill along with the sweet potato

and shishito pepper skewers, turning over once, until the potato slices are hot and lightly charred and the shishito peppers are charred and fully tender, about 10 minutes for the sweet potato and 4 minutes for the peppers. Meanwhile, grill the chicken skewers, turning and basting with more teriyaki sauce occasionally, until lightly charred, 2 to 5 minutes depending on the skewer.

Serve immediately with spice powder for sprinkling.

Note: When you thread the ingredients on the skewers, leave the bottom 2 inches of each skewer empty and make sure the tips are just barely sticking out (otherwise they could burn).

TSUKUNE NO TERIYAKI

CHICKEN MEATBALLS WITH TERIYAKI SAUCE

The secret to these scallion-studded chicken meatballs and what makes them the star of the yakitori *stage is the strange, wonderful mountain yam. Labeled in Asian markets as* nagaimo, yamaimo, *and Chinese yam, the ingredient has a slimy texture when grated that magically vanishes when mixed with ground chicken and grilled, leaving only a lovely, silky texture. That said, you can leave it out if you can't find it and still enjoy these sauce-slicked meatballs.*

MAKES ABOUT 18 MEATBALLS

Special Equipment
A grill (preferably charcoal)
6 bamboo skewers, soaked in water for 30 minutes
A food-safe brush

1 pound dark-meat ground chicken
¼ cup very finely chopped scallions (white and light green parts)
¼ cup finely grated peeled mountain yam (see Note)
2 tablespoons minced ginger
1 tablespoon sake (Japanese rice wine)
½ teaspoon kosher salt
2 large egg yolks
Ground white pepper to taste
Vegetable oil for the grill grates
½ cup teriyaki sauce (page 108)

PREPARE THE MEATBALLS

Bring a large pot of water to a boil.

Combine the chicken, scallions, yam, ginger, sake, salt, egg yolks, and white pepper in a small mixing bowl. Mix firmly with your hands until the ingredients are well distributed. The mixture will be much looser than that for the typical Western meatball.

One by one, form the meatballs and add them to the boiling water: spoon a generous tablespoon of the meatball mixture onto your palm, use the spoon to form it into an approximately 1½-inch ball, and carefully spoon it into the water. Cook until the meatballs are cooked through (they'll float to the surface and be firm to the touch), 6 to 8 minutes, using a slotted spoon to transfer them as they're done to a paper-towel-lined plate. You can grill them right away or let them cool and keep them covered in the fridge for up to 2 days. Let them come to room temperature before grilling.

GRILL THE MEATBALLS

Prepare the grill to cook over medium-high heat and lightly rub the grill grates with vegetable oil. Skewer the meatballs (about 3 per skewer) so that the bottom 2 inches of each skewer is empty and the tip is just barely sticking out from the top.

Generously brush the meatballs with teriyaki sauce and grill, turning over once and occasionally brushing on more sauce, until they're lightly charred, about 3 minutes. Serve immediately.

Note: Some people may experience a mild allergic reaction when handling mountain yam, so wear gloves when you peel and grate the yam.

SAKE SHIOYAKI

SALT-GRILLED SALMON

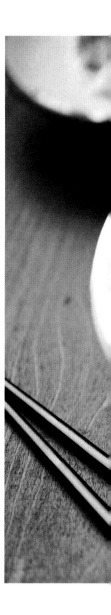

Sometimes another language's name for a dish makes it sound especially exotic and exciting. Take crudités for example. Much more appealing than "raw vegetables," right? Shioyaki, too, sounds exotic and special, and the dish certainly tastes extraordinary—crisp-skinned and flavor-packed. What could be the secret? Well, it's basically fish, seasoned with salt, and broiled. That's it!

The magic is in the details. Buy the best salmon you can lay your hands on (wild salmon delivers great flavor and texture) and ask your fishmonger (or beg, if you have to) for center-cut fillets with a strip of fatty belly attached. Then salt the fish an hour before you plan to cook, so the salt has a chance to penetrate the fish, not just season the exterior. Leftovers make a great filling for onigiri (rice balls, page 37), if you can leave fish this good uneaten.

SERVES 4

1½ pounds skin-on center-cut salmon fillet, cut crosswise into
    4 equal portions
2 tablespoons kosher salt
A drizzle of vegetable oil

Sprinkle the salt all over the fish. Let the fish sit uncovered in the refrigerator for 1 hour. Rinse off the salt and pat the fish dry.

Preheat the broiler and position the oven rack about 4 inches from the heat source. Drizzle a little vegetable oil on a baking sheet and rub to coat it with a very thin layer.

Arrange the fillets skin side down on the baking sheet, leaving some space between each one.

Broil, rotating the sheet once, until the fish is lightly browned and just cooked through, 4 to 6 minutes. Serve immediately.

MORIMOTO MAGIC TRICK: PROFESSIONAL COOKS IN JAPAN USE THIS NEAT TECHNIQUE CALLED *SAKAJIO* TO TONE DOWN A FISH'S, WELL, FISHINESS. TRY IT: BEFORE YOU START THIS RECIPE, STIR TOGETHER ¼ CUP PLUS 2 TABLESPOONS SAKE (JAPANESE RICE WINE) AND ½ TEASPOON KOSHER SALT IN A MEDIUM BOWL UNTIL THE SALT DISSOLVES. ONE BY ONE, ADD THE FISH FILLETS TO THE MIXTURE AND TAKE ABOUT 15 SECONDS OR SO TO TOSS THEM IN THE MIXTURE. PAT THE FILLETS DRY, PROCEED WITH THE RECIPE, AND MARVEL WHEN THE SALMON TASTES EVEN MORE LIKE, WELL, SALMON.

SAKANA NO MISOYAKI

Four ingredients. That's all it takes to re-create the famous flavors of miso-marinated black cod. Long ago, when I worked for Nobu Matsuhisa, I saw what is essentially a humble staple of Japanese grandmothers become an American sensation worth big bucks. Little did diners know, the dish is incredibly easy to make at home. Miso joins forces with sugar, sake, and mirin to infuse fish with unforgettable sweet-salty flavor, whether you're lucky enough to find buttery black cod or not. The marinade is so good that my recipe gives you three times the amount you need to make this dish, so in the weeks to come, you can use it to upgrade chicken and steak too.

SERVES 4

1 cup *shiro* (white) miso
1 cup granulated sugar
2 tablespoons sake (Japanese rice wine)
2 tablespoons mirin (sweet rice wine)
Four 4-ounce skin-on fatty white-fleshed fish fillets (½ to 1 inch thick), such as Spanish mackerel, black cod, or Chilean sea bass

MAKE THE MARINADE

Bring an inch of water to a boil in a small pot.

Combine the miso, sugar, sake, and mirin in a heatproof bowl that will fit in the small pot without touching the water, and whisk until smooth. Set the bowl in the pot and cook, stirring frequently, just until the grains of sugar in the marinade dissolve, about 5 minutes.

Let the mixture cool to room temperature. You'll have about 1½ cups of marinade and need only ½ cup for this recipe. In an airtight container, the marinade keeps for up to 2 weeks in the fridge or 1 month in the freezer.

MARINATE THE FISH

Pat the fillets dry and put them on a plate. Slather ½ cup of the marinade all over the fish. Cover with plastic wrap and marinate in the fridge for at least 8 hours or up to 12 hours.

COOK THE FISH

Preheat the oven to broil with an oven rack about 4 inches from the heating element.

Wipe off almost all of the marinade and discard it. Lightly oil a foil-lined baking sheet and arrange the fish skin side up with a little space between each one. Broil until the skin is browned all over and slightly charred in spots, about 5 minutes. Turn off the broiler and switch the oven to bake at 400°F. Continue to cook until the fish is just cooked through, 3 to 5 minutes more. Serve immediately.

NASU NO MISOYAKI

EGGPLANT WITH CHICKEN AND MISO SAUCE

Recently American chefs have started flipping their typical meat-vegetable ratio, giving vegetables a starring role while meat plays backup. This concept has already had a long life where I come from. It's a healthy, very Japanese way to eat. This recipe is one of my favorite examples: the deep-red miso sauce—as rich as any French sauce but without the butter or cream—brings out eggplant's natural sweetness, and a little ground chicken turns a perfect side dish into a hearty, satisfying meal.

SERVES 4

½ cup *aka* (red) miso
½ cup granulated sugar
½ cup plus 2 tablespoons sake (Japanese rice wine)
2 medium eggplants (about 2 pounds total), cut into
    1-inch-thick rounds
1 cup vegetable oil
½ pound dark meat ground chicken
A few pinches toasted sesame seeds (optional)

MAKE THE SAUCE

Bring an inch of water to a boil in a small pot.

Combine the miso, sugar, and ½ cup of the sake in a heatproof bowl that will fit in the small pot without touching the water and whisk until smooth. Set the bowl in the pot and cook, stirring and scraping the sides of the bowl occasionally, until the sauce has thickened slightly and the color has turned a shade darker, 15 to 20 minutes.

Set the bowl aside. In an airtight container, the sauce keeps for up to 1 week in the fridge.

MAKE THE DISH

Meanwhile, use a sharp knife to score both sides of the eggplant rounds every ¼ inch or so in a crosshatched pattern, going about ¼ inch into the flesh. Pour enough of the oil into a large nonstick skillet to reach a depth of ¼ inch and set the skillet over medium heat until the oil shimmers. Add half of the eggplant and cook, flipping the rounds once, until both sides are deep golden brown, the eggplant is cooked through, and some of the oil that the eggplant absorbed earlier releases back into the skillet, 8 to 10 minutes. Transfer to a paper towel to drain. Repeat with the remaining eggplant. When all the eggplant is cooked, discard all but 2 tablespoons of the oil, if necessary.

Increase the heat to medium-high, add the chicken to the oil, and cook, stirring and breaking up clumps, until it's just cooked through, about 3 minutes. Add the remaining 2 tablespoons sake and cook, stirring, until any liquid in the pan has evaporated, about 2 minutes. Take the skillet off the heat, stir in the miso sauce, and set the skillet over the heat again just until the miso begins to bubble.

Divide the eggplant among plates and spoon on the miso sauce. Sprinkle on the sesame seeds and serve right away.

TORI NO TERIYAKI

CHICKEN TERIYAKI

Ah, chicken teriyaki—so familiar, so rarely done right. Bottled products and mediocre restaurants have sullied the reputation of this fantastic dish. I can't wait until you try the real thing, which is lightly coated in a homemade sauce that's not goopy and saccharine, but thick and complexly sweet. In fact, the sauce provides such a boost that the grill isn't even necessary. The chicken turns out great on the stovetop.

SERVES 4

2 pounds boneless chicken thighs, breasts, or a mixture of the
    two
Kosher salt and black pepper
1 tablespoon vegetable oil
1½ teaspoons cornstarch
½ cup Tare No Teriyaki (teriyaki sauce, recipe follows)

If you're using chicken breasts, place a breast between 2 sheets of plastic wrap and pound it out to an even ½-inch thickness. Repeat with the remaining breasts. Lightly season both sides of the chicken with salt and black pepper.

Heat the oil in a large skillet over high heat until it shimmers. To avoid crowding the skillet, cook the chicken in 2 batches until deep golden brown on one side, about 6 minutes. Flip the chicken, reduce the heat to medium, and cook until just cooked through, 4 to 5 minutes more. Transfer the chicken to a plate as it's cooked.

In a small container, stir together the cornstarch and 1½ teaspoons water until smooth. Return half the chicken to the skillet and reduce the heat to medium. Pour in half of the *tare no teriyaki,* let it bubble, and drizzle on 1 teaspoon of the cornstarch mixture. Cook, flipping over the chicken often, until the sauce thickens and coats the chicken well, 1 to 2 minutes. Transfer the chicken to a cutting board and repeat.

Let the chicken rest for a few minutes, then cut into bite-size pieces. Serve right away or keep refrigerated in an airtight container and serve it in your bento box the following day.

Tare No Teriyaki

TERIYAKI SAUCE

Teriyaki has become as common in America as tacos and General Tso's. Yet like those other famous foreign T-words, the dish is so much better than its many impostors lead you to believe. The key is the sauce, which takes minutes to make and keeps well. My version boasts extra complexity from ginger and garlic.

MAKES ABOUT 1½ CUPS

½ cup Japanese soy sauce
½ cup mirin (sweet rice wine)
½ cup sake (Japanese rice wine)
½ cup granulated sugar
¼ cup roughly chopped yellow onion
5 thin round slices peeled ginger
2 medium garlic cloves, smashed and peeled

Combine the ingredients in a small pot, bring to a boil over high heat, and reduce the heat to maintain a gentle simmer. Cook for about 8 minutes so the aromatics have a chance to infuse their flavor into the liquid. Strain, discarding the solids.

The sauce keeps in an airtight container in the fridge for up to 2 weeks.

GYOZA

PORK AND CABBAGE DUMPLINGS

I bet you've enjoyed these pork dumplings, golden brown on the bottom and juicy inside, at one of the 99.9 percent of Japanese restaurants in America that serve them. But I bet you haven't tried making them yourself. It ensures truly exceptional dumplings and some serious fun. Invite friends to join in, and everyone can try his or her hand at folding the wrappers into pleats. They not only look pretty—the more pleats, the more skilled the dumpling maker—they also act as reinforcement, making the skins less likely to break while they cook.

MAKES ABOUT 24 DUMPLINGS

Special Equipment
Cheesecloth

For the Filling
4 cups finely chopped napa cabbage
1½ cups very thinly sliced garlic chives, or 1½ cups thinly
    sliced scallions plus 1 teaspoon minced garlic
1 tablespoon plus ½ teaspoon kosher salt
½ pound fatty ground pork, such as shoulder or belly
1 tablespoon sake (Japanese rice wine)
1½ teaspoons toasted sesame oil
Ground white pepper to taste

For the Dumplings
About 24 *gyoza* wrappers or "Shanghai-style" round dumpling
    wrappers
2 tablespoons vegetable oil

For the Sauce
3 tablespoons Japanese soy sauce
3 tablespoons unseasoned rice vinegar
Japanese hot mustard to taste
1 tablespoon thinly sliced scallion greens

MAKE THE FILLING

Combine the cabbage and garlic chives (or scallions and garlic, if using) in a medium mixing bowl. Sprinkle on 1 tablespoon of the salt, toss very well, and let the mixture sit for 15 minutes or so. Rinse the cabbage mixture under running water, then use your hands to squeeze the mixture to release some of the liquid. Transfer the mixture to two layers of cheesecloth or a clean kitchen towel and squeeze out and discard as much liquid as you can.

Combine the cabbage mixture, pork, sake, sesame oil, white pepper, and the remaining ½ teaspoon salt in a medium mixing bowl. Firmly mix with your hands until the ingredients are well distributed and the mixture is slightly sticky to the touch.

FORM THE DUMPLINGS

Line a large plate or tray with parchment paper. Fill a small bowl with water. Form one dumpling at a time, keeping unused wrappers covered with a kitchen towel and transferring the finished dumplings to the parchment paper.

Spoon 1 tablespoon of the filling onto the center of a wrapper. Dip a finger or brush into the water and moisten the edge of the wrapper. Fold the wrapper over the filling and firmly pinch one of the corners so the sides of

the wrapper stick together. Enclose the filling, making 4 pleats (as shown on pages 110–11). Firmly squeeze the pleated edge.

You can form the dumplings up to 4 hours in advance if you cover the tray with plastic wrap and keep it in the fridge.

COOK THE DUMPLINGS

Heat 1 tablespoon of the oil in a large nonstick skillet with a lid over medium heat until it shimmers. Put the dumplings pleats side up in the skillet next to one another (a pinwheel arrangement will maximize space). Pour in enough water to reach about halfway up the sides of the dumplings, increase the heat to high, and cover the skillet.

Cook for 5 minutes, then remove the lid, reduce the heat to medium-high, and cook, swirling the liquid around the pan occasionally, until the water remaining in the pan looks thick and cloudy, about 1 minute. Drizzle the remaining 1 tablespoon oil over the dumplings, decrease the heat to medium, and continue cooking, uncovered, until the bottoms are brown and crispy, 5 to 8 minutes.

Meanwhile, stir together the soy sauce, rice vinegar, mustard, and scallion until well combined and set aside. Transfer the dumplings browned side up to a plate or platter and serve immediately with the sauce in bowls for dipping.

TAMAGOYAKI

JAPANESE OMELET

Often called a Japanese omelet, this slightly sweet, custardy marvel might confuse anyone expecting the savory, fluffy, herb-flecked Western version. Yet one bite will turn you into a devotee. The magic is in the method, which creates many layers of eggy goodness. Most cooks use a kotobuki tamagoyaki, *a special pan made for this dish, which you can have shipped to your door for just $20.*

Great warm for dinner or cold in a bento box the next day, tamagoyaki is one example of Japanese home cooking that takes a little time and practice to get right. But even your first attempt will impress your friends, and you'll get better and better each time you cook it.

SERVES 4

Special Equipment
One approximately 7 by 5-inch *tamagoyaki* pan (highly
    recommended)

¼ cup plus 2 tablespoons Dashi (dried fish and kelp stock,
    page 20) or Kombu Dashi (kelp stock, page 23), warm
1 teaspoon *usukuchi* (Japanese light-colored soy sauce)
1 tablespoon granulated sugar
4 large eggs, beaten
Vegetable oil

Combine the dashi, soy sauce, and sugar in a large bowl and stir until the sugar has dissolved. Add the eggs to the bowl and beat to combine well. Set a medium-mesh sieve over a measuring cup with a spout and pour in the egg mixture. Strain the mixture, stirring to get most of the liquid through, leaving just about a tablespoon of the thick whites in the sieve.

Set the *tamagoyaki* pan or an 8-inch nonstick skillet over medium heat. Let it get hot for a few minutes. Pour a tablespoon or two of the oil into a small bowl. Dip a folded paper towel into the oil and briefly rub the surface and sides of the pan. Keep the paper towel nearby.

Pour into the pan just enough of the egg mixture (about 3 tablespoons)

to cover the surface and immediately swirl the egg mixture so it covers the bottom in a thin layer, pushing down any egg that sticks to the sides. Use the edge of a nonmetal spatula (or, if you're like me, chopsticks) to pop any little bubbles that appear. Let the egg cook, without stirring, just until it sets, about 20 seconds. Take the pan off the heat, tilt the handle down, and use a nonmetal spatula to gently fold the egg forward in half onto itself.

Set the pan back on the heat. Rub the empty space at the back of the pan with oil, then slide the cooked egg, using the spatula to help if need be, into the empty space. Rub the now-empty space in the front of the pan with oil.

Pour about 3 tablespoons more of the egg mixture into the empty space, tilting the pan and slightly lifting the cooked egg so the liquidy egg runs underneath it. Cook until the raw egg has just set, 30 to 45 seconds. Take the pan off the heat, tilt the handle down, and use a spatula to gently fold the egg forward in half onto itself.

Set the pan back on the heat again and repeat the process until you've used all of the egg mixture. If the omelet is not by this point golden brown in spots on both sides, cook over medium heat for a few minutes on each side. Transfer the omelet to a cutting board, let it cool slightly, and slice it crosswise into ¾-inch-thick slices. Serve warm.

Wrapped in plastic wrap, the omelet keeps in the fridge for up to 2 days. When you're ready to serve, transfer the omelet to a cutting board and slice it crosswise into ¾-inch-thick slices.

BUTA NO SHOGAYAKI

PORK BELLY WITH GINGER AND ONIONS

You can't get much simpler than this lunchtime classic, the rice topper of your dreams: a handful of ingredients, a very brief marinade, and a quick trip in a hot pan. Once it's done, the sugar and mirin have helped the pork caramelize, the sharp ginger cuts through the sweetness, and you can barely resist demolishing all four servings in one sitting. Fans of the rich flavor and slightly chewy texture of pork belly should embrace their craving, though even lean pork loin hits the spot.

SERVES 4

3 tablespoons Japanese soy sauce
2 tablespoons mirin (sweet rice wine)
2 teaspoons finely grated ginger
1 teaspoon granulated sugar
1 pound thinly sliced pork belly or shoulder (see Thinly Slicing Meat at Home, opposite)
½ medium yellow onion, cut with the grain into ½-inch-thick slices
2 tablespoons vegetable oil

Combine the soy sauce, mirin, ginger, and sugar in a medium mixing bowl and stir until the sugar dissolves. Add the pork and onion and toss to coat them well. Let the pork marinate at room temperature for 10 minutes.

Heat the oil in a large nonstick or well-seasoned cast-iron skillet over high heat until it shimmers. Add half of the pork mixture in a single layer and cook without stirring, occasionally pressing the pork pieces so they lie flat, until the slices have begun to brown, about 2 minutes. Transfer to a bowl (the meat will not be fully cooked). Add the remaining pork mixture in a single layer. Cook in the same way. When it has browned, return the pork from the bowl to the pan and continue to cook, stirring, until all the pork is cooked through, 1 to 2 minutes. Serve right away.

THINLY SLICING MEAT AT HOME

Japanese markets sell thinly sliced meat including pork belly and beef, and many butchers will slice meat for you if you ask nicely. If all else fails, you can slice it yourself: just wrap it in plastic and freeze until very firm, about 30 minutes, then thinly slice against the grain into approximately 4-inch-long pieces. They should look like shorter slices of bacon.

JAPANESE GRANDMOTHER WISDOM

Pork belly is rich, and that's exactly why I love it. Fat means flavor, and plenty of it makes this dish hard to resist. Yet there's a difference between pleasantly fatty and distractingly greasy. To make sure your *buta no shogayaki* never crosses this line, try this: Before you transfer the dish to a plate, fold a paper towel to form a tight bundle. Use tongs or long chopsticks to grab the bundle and spend thirty seconds or so patting the pork and the skillet to soak up the excess fat.

MUSU 蒸す

To steam

Remember when the word *steamed* entered the American culinary vocabulary? It immediately became a synonym for "healthy," and all of a sudden steamers were the latest must-have kitchen gadgets. You could tell Americans were new to the ritual, because they did little more than steam vegetables, then choke them down. I could only chuckle, because we Japanese have known the magic of steaming for centuries. And lots of practice produces seriously delicious dishes that don't ditch the flavor with the oil. My wife, Keiko, is a genius with a steamer, and I have them both to thank for my forty-pound weight loss.

SAKANA NO SAKAMUSHI

FISH STEAMED IN KOMBU WITH SPICY SOY SAUCE

The spicy sauce might be what tempts you to make this dish, but believe me, this recipe is all about the fish. The quick bath in sake and salt washes away any distracting fishiness. The kombu wrapping protects the delicate fillets from the heat and imbues them with umami. The result flaunts the best that the fish has to offer. The sauce makes each bite exciting.

SERVES 4

Special Equipment
A noncollapsible metal steamer insert or a 10-inch bamboo
    steamer and parchment paper or cheesecloth

For the Sauce
¼ cup Japanese soy sauce
1½ tablespoons unseasoned rice vinegar
1½ tablespoons finely chopped scallions (white and light
    green parts)
1 tablespoon granulated sugar
1½ teaspoons mirin (sweet rice wine)
1½ teaspoons toasted sesame oil
1½ teaspoons *tobanjan* (chile bean sauce), preferably a
    Japanese brand
1 teaspoon toasted sesame seeds

For the Fish
1 very large or 2 large pieces kombu (dried kelp), soaked in
    cold water for 15 minutes until pliable and cut to make
    four 7 by 5-inch rectangles
¼ cup plus 2 tablespoons sake (Japanese rice wine)
½ teaspoon salt
Four 5-ounce skin-on fatty white fish fillets, such as
    Spanish mackerel, black cod, or Chilean sea bass

MAKE THE SAUCE

Combine the sauce ingredients in a small bowl and stir well.

STEAM AND SERVE THE FISH

Lay the 4 rectangles of kombu on a cutting board. Stir together the sake and salt in a medium bowl until the salt dissolves. One by one, add the fish fillets to the sake mixture and take 15 seconds or so to turn them over so each side spends some time in the mixture. Add each fillet to a piece of kombu and fold and roll the kombu around the fish to form a rough cylinder with two open ends.

Prepare the steamer, either a pot with a metal steamer insert or a bamboo steamer set over a skillet. If you're using a steamer insert, rub the surface lightly with vegetable oil. If you're using a bamboo steamer, line the surface with cheesecloth or parchment paper. Pour about 1 inch of water into the pot or skillet. Bring the water to a boil, then reduce the heat slightly to maintain a slightly less rapid boil. Add the fish, cover, and cook until just cooked through, about 10 minutes.

Divide the kombu-wrapped fish among 4 plates, unwrap, spoon on the sauce, and serve right away.

SHUMAI

JAPANESE-STYLE SHRIMP DUMPLINGS

In the refrigerated section of Japanese supermarkets and convenience stores lurks a fraud, a phony, a sham—the strangely sweet, leaden dumplings that claim to be shumai. The real thing is almost unrecognizable. Shrimp contribute their sea-sweet flavor and springy texture, and a little pork fat (in this case, bacon) keeps the filling juicy and full of flavor. You don't have to reveal to your guests that shumai are as easy to form as they are impressive to behold.

MAKES ABOUT 20 DUMPLINGS

Special Equipment
A noncollapsible metal steamer insert or a bamboo steamer
    and parchment paper or cheesecloth

For the Filling
¾ pound shelled white shrimp, deveined
½ cup diced (about ¼ inch) yellow onion
2 teaspoons cornstarch
½ cup finely diced fresh shiitake mushroom caps
⅓ cup diced (about ¼ inch) fatty bacon
1 tablespoon finely chopped scallions (white and light green
    parts)
1 large egg white
1 tablespoon sake (Japanese rice wine)
1 teaspoon finely chopped ginger
1 teaspoon kosher salt
1 teaspoon granulated sugar
1 teaspoon toasted sesame oil

For the Dumplings
20 *shumai* skins or "Shanghai-style" round dumpling wrappers
20 fresh or defrosted frozen shelled edamame
Vegetable oil
Shumai Sauce for serving (recipe follows)

(Recipe continues on page 130)

(Continued from page 125)

MAKE THE FILLING

Pulse the shrimp in a food processor until you have a very chunky paste. (You can also smash the shrimp one at a time with the flat part of a cleaver, then roughly chop them.) Combine the onion and cornstarch in a medium bowl and toss to coat. Add the shrimp and the remaining ingredients to the bowl with the onion. Stir very roughly with your hands until the mixture is slightly sticky and clumps together, at least 30 seconds.

Steady the bowl with one hand and pick up a big handful of the mixture, then forcefully slap it against the bowl (this removes air and helps give the dumplings a slightly dense texture). Repeat once or twice, then do the same with the rest of the mixture.

FORM THE DUMPLINGS

Line a large plate or tray with parchment paper. Fill a small bowl with water. Form one dumpling at a time, keeping unused wrappers covered with a kitchen towel and transferring the finished dumplings to the parchment paper. (See the step-by-step photos on pages 126–127.)

Spoon a generous tablespoon of the filling onto the center of a wrapper. Spread it slightly so it sticks to the wrapper, leaving an approximately ¼-inch border. Gather up the edges of the wrapper with both hands so that it resembles a flower. Transfer it to one hand, gently cupping it to stabilize the sides while you use your other hand to gently flatten and compress the filling with a small spoon. Set the dumpling down onto the parchment paper, holding the sides up for a few seconds to help set the shape. Top with an edamame and repeat with the remaining wrappers and filling.

STEAM THE DUMPLINGS

Prepare the steamer, either a pot with a metal steamer insert or a bamboo steamer set over a skillet. If you're using a steamer insert, rub the surface lightly with vegetable oil. If you're using a bamboo steamer, line the surface with cheesecloth or parchment paper.

Pour about 1 inch of water into the pot or skillet. Bring the water to a boil, then reduce the heat slightly to maintain a slightly less rapid boil. Add the *shumai* to the steamer in a single layer, leaving about ½ inch of space between each one. Set the steamer in the pot or skillet, cover, and steam until the filling is cooked through (the shrimp will be opaque with pink patches), about 8 minutes.

Transfer the *shumai* to a plate and serve with the dipping sauce (see Note).

Note: Shumai can be cooked, cooled to room temperature, and refrigerated (covered) for up to 2 hours. Rewarm in the steamer until heated through, about 4 minutes. Shumai can also be frozen raw in an airtight container and kept up to 2 weeks. Steam directly from frozen until cooked through, about 10 minutes.

Shumai Sauce

MAKES ENOUGH FOR ABOUT 20 DUMPLINGS

3 tablespoons Japanese soy sauce
3 tablespoons unseasoned rice vinegar
Japanese or Chinese mustard paste to taste
Asian chile oil to taste

Combine the soy sauce, vinegar, mustard paste, and chile oil in a bowl and stir well.

CHAWANMUSHI

EGG CUSTARD WITH SHRIMP, CHICKEN, AND FISH

I grew up loving this egg custard, rooting around for all the treats—the shrimp, the gingko nut!—hiding at the bottom. I adored it even though my mother almost always messed it up. She was an impatient cook and lacked the discipline to maintain gentle heat, so her version was as dense as an omelet. Later in life, I came to love chawanmushi *even more when I learned that the proper texture is featherweight and impossibly delicate, like a savory panna cotta. If you're freaked out by the idea of making custard, have no fear, Morimoto is here!*

SERVES 4

Special Equipment
4 small heatproof bowls or 8-ounce ramekins
Parchment paper or cheesecloth

3 cups Dashi (dried fish and kelp stock, page 20) or Kombu Dashi (kelp stock, page 23)
1 tablespoon plus 1 teaspoon *usukuchi* (Japanese light-colored soy sauce), plus 1 tablespoon
2 teaspoons mirin (sweet rice wine)
½ teaspoon kosher salt
4 large eggs
8 thin, bite-size slices boneless skinless chicken thigh (from 1 small thigh)
One 3-ounce fillet delicate white-fleshed fish, such as fluke or flounder, cut into 8 thin bite-size slices
4 medium shrimp, peeled and deveined
8 drained canned gingko nuts or 4 jarred or vacuum-packed roasted chestnuts, halved
¼ cup loosely packed very roughly chopped mitsuba or thinly sliced scallions

Combine the dashi, 1 tablespoon plus 1 teaspoon of the *usukuchi*, the mirin, and salt in a small pot, bring to a boil, then let cool completely.

Gently mix the eggs in a medium bowl so they're well mixed but don't develop bubbles. Pour in the dashi mixture, stir well, then strain into a measuring cup, discarding any solids.

Briefly toss the chicken, fish, and shrimp in a bowl with the remaining 1 tablespoon soy sauce, shake to let any excess drip off, and divide them among the 4 small bowls or ramekins. Divide the gingko nuts among the bowls or ramekins, then divide the egg mixture evenly among them and cover with foil.

Line a wide, shallow-lidded pot or a Dutch oven with a paper towel. Add 1 inch of water and bring to a boil over high heat. Carefully add the bowls to the pot and cover with the lid. Cook until the custard turns pale, 3 to 4 minutes, then carefully remove the bowls from the pot. Add the mitsuba or scallion to the surface of the custard and re-cover with the foil.

Reduce the heat to maintain a gentle simmer, return the bowls to the water, and cover the pot with the lid so it's slightly ajar. Cook until the custard is just set but still jiggles when you shake the bowls (or a skewer inserted into the middle comes out clean), 12 to 15 minutes. Serve immediately.

NIRU

煮る

To simmer

Simmered doesn't sound very exciting, does it? It certainly doesn't entice like the words *charred* and *broiled* do. Well, simmering the Japanese way should get you salivating, because it produces some of my favorite dishes of all. The secret is creating a cooking liquid that highlights the flavor of the main ingredient and strikes the right balance between sweet and salty. And the best part is that enchanted Japanese pantry staples like sake, mirin, and soy sauce give you more flavor than Western stews, often in a fraction of the time. Learn to simmer the Japanese way, and you might never go back.

THE SIMMERING SECRET: OTOSHIBUTA

If you peek over my shoulder while I'm simmering, you'll likely see a wooden disc in the bubbling liquid. This inexpensive, special device is called *otoshibuta* (or "drop lid," in English), and it's up there with my knives as one of the most important tools in my kitchen.

Unlike a standard lid, the *otoshibuta* is slightly smaller than the width of the pan or pot it rests in. And instead of rising above the rim, it sits on the surface. This serves several purposes. Because the *otoshibuta* doesn't completely cover the liquid, it allows the liquid to slowly evaporate, getting more concentrated and delicious. Yet as some of that liquid hits the lid and drops back down onto the ingredients you're simmering, it essentially bastes them and keeps them moist. This way, you can cook with a relatively small amount of liquid instead of submerging the ingredients. And it means you don't have to turn or stir the ingredients, which could break them.

If you can spare $15, you should buy a wooden *otoshibuta* online or at an Asian cookware store. (Soak it in cold water for 10 minutes before each use, so it doesn't absorb your delicious simmering liquid.) But in case you're wondering, yes, you can certainly simmer the Japanese way without one. Frequent basting is one option, but I prefer to fashion a disposable *otoshibuta* out of foil or parchment paper. Just tear off a large piece of foil and crimp the edges in order to make a sturdy round that's about 2 inches smaller in diameter than your skillet or pot. For parchment paper, cut a circle that's about 2 inches smaller in diameter, then cut a small circle (about ½ inch) from the center. This allows a little steam to escape, so the parchment won't puff up but rather lies on the surface, like a real *otoshibuta.*

SABA NO MISONI

MACKEREL SIMMERED WITH MISO

Grilling gets all the glory. But this Japanese-grandma staple proves that simmering is a tragically underappreciated way of cooking fish. Virtually any fish benefits from a brief trip in bubbling miso, though mackerel— slightly oily, so it's both flavorful and forgiving, not to mention healthful and inexpensive—is my fish of choice. The result is boldly flavored, so make sure you eat it with plenty of rice or plenty of glasses of sake.

SERVES 4

Special Equipment
A wooden *otoshibuta* or one made from foil (see page 139)

¼ cup *shiro* (white) miso or *aka* (red) miso
¼ cup granulated sugar
1 cup sake (Japanese rice wine)
Two 3-inch pieces scallion (preferably from the light
    green portion)
Four ¼-inch-thick coins peeled ginger
Four 3-ounce Atlantic or Spanish mackerel fillets, rinsed
    well, patted dry, and halved crosswise

Combine the miso and sugar in a small bowl and stir well.

Combine the sake, scallion, ginger, and ½ cup water in a skillet wide enough to fit the fillets in a single layer with room to spare. Bring to a boil over high heat, spoon a few tablespoons of the boiling liquid into the bowl with the miso, and stir until the mixture is smooth. Add the miso mixture to the skillet, stir, then add the fillets flesh side down in a single layer.

Spend about 1 minute basting the fillets (tipping the pan and spooning the liquid over the fillets). Cover with the *otoshibuta*. Cook, adjusting the heat to maintain a strong simmer, until the liquid has thickened and becomes slightly glossy, 10 to 12 minutes.

Remove the *otoshibuta,* reduce the heat to medium, and continue cooking, occasionally shaking the pan to make sure the fish doesn't stick or burn and frequently tipping the pan and basting, until the liquid thickly coats the fillets and there are only a couple of tablespoons remaining in the pan, about 8 minutes more.

Transfer the fish to plates and spoon on the remaining sauce. Let cool slightly before serving.

NITSUKE

FISH SIMMERED WITH SAKE, SOY SAUCE, AND SUGAR

Even my mother made a pretty good nitsuke—*that's how easy this dish is to cook. Because it takes only a little extra effort and adds a ton of flavor, I like to break with tradition and reduce the cooking liquid into a more intensely flavorful sauce.*

SERVES 4

Special Equipment
A wooden *otoshibuta* or one made from foil (see page 139)

1½ cups Dashi (dried fish and kelp stock, page 20), Kombu Dashi (kelp stock, page 23), or water
½ cup sake (Japanese rice wine)
½ cup mirin (sweet rice wine)
¼ cup plus 2 tablespoons Japanese soy sauce
1 tablespoon granulated sugar
Four ¼-inch-thick coins peeled ginger
Four 4-ounce skin-on fillets fatty white-fleshed fish, such as Spanish mackerel, redfish, Chilean sea bass, or black cod
¼ pound drained medium-firm tofu, cut into 4 equal pieces

Combine the dashi, sake, mirin, soy sauce, sugar, and ginger in a medium skillet and bring to a boil. Add the fish skin side up in a single layer and cover with the *otoshibuta*. Reduce the heat and simmer for about 12 minutes. The fish will be fully cooked after about 8 minutes; the longer cooking time infuses the fish with the flavor of the cooking liquid.

Remove the *otoshibuta,* carefully transfer the fish to a plate, and increase the heat to high to bring the liquid to a boil. Add the tofu to the skillet and cook, flipping once, until the liquid reduces slightly and its flavor intensifies, 8 to 10 minutes.

Return the fish to the skillet and continue cooking, basting constantly with a spoon, for a minute or two. Serve right away in shallow bowls with some of the cooking liquid. Or even better, remove from the heat, cover with the *otoshibuta* or partially with a lid, and let the fish sit for 10 to 15 minutes, so the fish absorbs even more flavor from the sauce.

HAMBAGU

JAPANESE-STYLE HAMBURGER WITH TANGY SAUCE

Soon after my famously introverted home country opened itself to the West in the mid-nineteenth century, a sub-cuisine known as yoshoku *was born. Yoshoku is essentially Western dishes cooked from the Japanese perspective, and today its popularity rivals that of sushi. The* hambagu *is a prime example, a burger patty–meat loaf hybrid—think Salisbury steak doused with ketchup-spiked teriyaki instead of gravy and served with rice instead of mashed potatoes—enlivened by the alchemy of the Japanese pantry. The concept might have started in the West, but the dish has become as Japanese as I am.*

MAKES 4 HAMBURGERS

1 tablespoon unsalted butter
1 medium yellow onion, very finely diced
½ cup panko breadcrumbs
¼ cup plus 2 tablespoons whole milk
1 pound ground beef (preferably 80% lean)
1 teaspoon kosher salt
½ teaspoon freshly grated nutmeg
White pepper to taste
1 large egg
1 tablespoon vegetable oil, plus extra for your hands
1 cup teriyaki sauce (page 108)
¼ cup ketchup
2 teaspoons Dijon mustard

Heat a medium skillet over medium-high heat, add the butter, and let it melt. Add the onion and cook, stirring frequently, until the onion is translucent and light brown at the edges, about 8 minutes. Let the onion cool. Meanwhile, combine the panko and milk in a medium bowl, stir to moisten the crumbs, and let the mixture sit for 5 minutes or so.

Add the onion, beef, salt, nutmeg, and white pepper to the bowl with the panko mixture and mix firmly with your hands until the ingredients are well distributed and the mixture is slightly sticky to the touch, about 1 minute. Add the egg and mix again, about 30 seconds more.

Using lightly oiled hands, grab about a quarter of the meat mixture and firmly toss it back and forth between your hands for about 1 minute, or 30 seconds if you're quick. (The goal—unlike that of most Western hamburger makers—is to get rid of most of the air hiding out in the

patties.) Form 4 patties of more or less equal size (about 4½ inches in diameter and ½ inch thick). Use your fingers to make a gently sloping dent in the center of each patty; this way, they won't puff too much during cooking.

Heat 1 tablespoon of the oil in a large skillet over medium-high heat until it begins to smoke. Add the patties, leaving a little space between each one, and cook until the undersides are deep golden brown, 2 to 3 minutes. Lower the heat to medium, flip over the patties, and cook until the undersides are browned, about 3 minutes more.

Meanwhile, stir together the teriyaki sauce, ketchup, and mustard in a small bowl and add the mixture to the skillet. Let the sauce come to a gentle simmer and cook, flipping the patties occasionally, until they are cooked to medium or medium well, 3 to 5 minutes. Serve right away.

BUTA NO KAKUNI

SLOW-COOKED PORK BELLY WITH
BEER-TERIYAKI GLAZE

*Few things on earth are as decadent as pork belly slowly simmered until you can
cut it with chopsticks. So many cuisines have their renditions, but it'll come as no
surprise that I enjoy the Japanese one most of all. By the time the pork is finished,
the cooking liquid—nontraditionally but deliciously, it's just teriyaki sauce
and beer!—has reduced to a thick sweet-salty sauce that could make a baseball
mitt taste great. I prefer cooking kakuni in two stages: the first quiets the pork's
gaminess and starts it down the road to tenderness, while the second infuses
the meat with flavor and completes the textural transformation. Kaku means
"square" and refers to the eye-catching presentation of the belly, so try your best to
cut pieces with flat edges and sharp corners.*

SERVES 6

Special Equipment
A wooden *otoshibuta* or one made from foil (see page 139)

One 2-pound piece pork belly
A generous handful of raw brown rice
1 cup teriyaki sauce (page 108)
One 12-ounce bottle light-colored, mild beer such as pilsner
   or lager

6 TO 48 HOURS BEFORE YOU PLAN TO SERVE

Preheat a large skillet over medium heat, add the pork, and cook, turning
over occasionally and draining the fat once, until it's light golden brown
on both sides, 10 to 15 minutes.

Transfer the pork to a medium pot, add enough water to cover it by
2 inches, then add the brown rice. Bring to a boil over medium-high heat,
then reduce the heat to maintain a gentle simmer and cook, flipping the
pork over once, until a skewer or sharp knife goes into the pork easily,
about 2 hours. Drain well, discarding the rice.

Transfer the pork to a plate and let cool to room temperature. If not cooking right away, tightly wrap the plate and pork with plastic wrap. This will prevent curling and help the pork stay flat. You can keep it in the fridge for up to 2 days.

THE DAY YOU PLAN TO SERVE

Trim the pork so the edges are flat (optional). Cut the pork belly into 6 equal-size portions, preferably square portions. Put the pork fat side down in a medium skillet, pour in the teriyaki sauce and beer, and bring to a simmer over medium-high heat.

Cover with the *otoshibuta* and cook, flipping once about halfway through and adjusting the heat to maintain a simmer, until the liquid has thickened to a consistency slightly thinner than maple syrup and the pork is tender enough to cut with chopsticks, 1¼ to 1½ hours.

You can eat it right away or, even better, leave it in the pot for a couple of hours, then warm it very gently before serving.

JAPANESE GRANDMOTHER WISDOM

Oops, you might say to yourself, someone accidentally spilled raw rice into the pot with the pork belly. But it was no accident. Adding a generous handful of raw rice, brown or white, to the water along with the pork belly is a time-honored way to remove the strong, gamy quality of the meat. The result is a purer, more lovable porky flavor.

CHIKUZENNI

CHICKEN SIMMERED WITH LOTUS ROOT AND BAMBOO SHOOT

Once a dish prepared mainly during the first few days of the New Year, chikuzenni is so tasty that it has become everyday food. I know I can't wait until January to dig into this vegetable-heavy, sauceless chicken stew. As usual, little more than dashi stock and a couple of pantry ingredients team up to make a humble, healthful collection of ingredients taste special. The most festive versions feature carrots and lotus root carved into cute shapes, but your guests will love yours whether or not your carrots resemble little flowers.

SERVES 4 TO 6

¼ pound vacuum-packed precooked bamboo shoot (*takenoko*)
¼ pound vacuum-packed precooked lotus root (*renkon*)
½ cup trimmed, cut (about 1-inch lengths) green beans
½ cup trimmed, halved snowpeas
Eight 3-inch-long, ¼-inch-thick slices drained gray *konnyaku* (Japanese "yam cake")
2 tablespoons toasted sesame oil
¾ pound boneless chicken thighs, cut into 1½-inch pieces
1½ cups roughly chopped (into irregular 1-inch pieces) peeled carrots
6 medium dried shiitake mushroom caps, rehydrated (page 254) and quartered
2 cups Dashi (dried fish and kelp stock, page 20) or Kombu Dashi (kelp stock, page 23)
¼ cup plus 2 tablespoons Japanese soy sauce
¼ cup mirin (sweet rice wine)
2 tablespoons granulated sugar

Drain the bamboo shoot and lotus root. Trim the bumpy exterior from the base of the bamboo shoot. Cut each into ¾-inch pieces.

Bring a medium pot of water to a boil. Add the green beans and snowpeas and cook for 2 minutes. Scoop them out and rinse them well under cold water. Drain well and transfer to a bowl. Add the lotus root, bamboo shoot, and *konnyaku* to the boiling water, cook for 1 minute, then drain in a colander.

Because *chikuzenni* began as celebratory food, cooks took time to show off their carving skills on the carrot and lotus root. You might not want to try this at home, but you should try this easy way to add a little flair to your version of the dish: One by one, lay a 3-inch-long slice of *konnyaku* on a cutting board or plate, and use the tip of a knife to make a 2-inch-long slit along the center, leaving about ½ inch at both ends of the slit intact. Carefully open the slit, fold one of the short ends through the slit, and pull gently to create a cool coil shape that only looks like it was hard to make.

Combine the sesame oil and chicken in a large skillet and set it over medium-high heat. Cook, stirring occasionally, just until the chicken is no longer pink on the outside, about 3 minutes.

Add the lotus root, bamboo shoot, *konnyaku,* carrots, and mushrooms and cook, stirring, for 1 minute. Add the dashi, let it come to a boil, and cook for 3 minutes. Stir in the soy sauce, mirin, and sugar and bring to a boil. Cook at a boil, tossing occasionally, until the liquid has completely evaporated, about 20 minutes.

Add the green beans and snowpeas, toss well, and transfer to bowls. Let the dish cool slightly before serving. It keeps in an airtight container in the fridge for up to 3 days.

NIKUJAGA

JAPANESE-STYLE BEEF STEW

I remember eating pot roast for the first time when I came to America and wondering where the flavor was. In Japan, we too ate simple stews of beef and potatoes, but they were bold bowlfuls that made me crave more and more rice to eat with every last trace of soupy sauce. Made from the holy trinity of Japanese bottled seasonings—soy sauce, sake, and mirin—it gives even the French trio of red wine, butter, and thyme a serious run for its money. Not only is this dish even better the next day, it's so much better that I highly recommend making it a day or two before you eat it.

SERVES 4

4 cups Dashi (dried fish and kelp stock, page 20) or Kombu Dashi (kelp stock, page 23)
2 tablespoons sake (Japanese rice wine)
2 tablespoons mirin (sweet rice wine)
2 cups roughly chopped (into irregular 1-inch pieces) peeled potatoes
1 cup roughly chopped (into irregular 1-inch pieces) peeled carrots
4 spring onion bulbs (about 1 inch in diameter), trimmed and first layer of skin discarded
1 cup drained *shirataki* (noodles made from *konjac,* or yam)
½ pound very thinly sliced rib eye or chuck eye roll (see Note)
¼ cup Japanese soy sauce
2 tablespoons granulated sugar

Combine the dashi, sake, mirin, potatoes, carrots, and spring onions in a medium pot and bring the liquid to a boil over high heat. Cook at a boil until the carrots are tender but still have a slight bite, about 10 minutes.

Meanwhile, bring a small pot of water to a boil. Put the *shirataki* in a mesh strainer and set the strainer in the boiling water. Cook, stirring once, for 10 seconds. Keep the water at a boil. Run the *shirataki* under cold water, drain them well, and very roughly chop them. Add the beef to the water and cook, stirring with tongs, just until it's no longer pink, about 10 seconds. Drain the beef.

When the 10 minutes have passed, add the beef, *shirataki,* soy sauce, and sugar to the pot with the vegetables. Reduce the heat to maintain a simmer and cook until the potatoes are fully tender, 8 to 10 minutes. Remove the stew from the heat, let it cool to room temperature, then refrigerate for at least 6 hours or up to 3 days.

When ready to serve, reheat gently, covered, until the vegetables are hot through.

Note: Look for thinly sliced beef at Japanese markets, often labeled shabu shabu *or* sukiyaki, *or slice it yourself (see Thinly Slicing Meat at Home, page 119).*

HIJIKI

SWEET SIMMERED HIJIKI SEAWEED

Seaweed fans and skeptics all love hijiki. *Fans eat up the aquatic vegetable's especially high calcium and iron content, while skeptics are won over by its meaty texture (it lacks the slippery quality they associate with other seaweeds) and neutral flavor (by the time it's cooked,* hijiki *tastes like the wonderful sweet-salty cooking liquid). And no one minds that* hijiki *takes very little effort to cook and keeps for days in the fridge.*

SERVES 4

½ cup dried *hijiki* (preferably *me hijiki;* see Note)
1 tablespoon toasted sesame oil
½ cup carrot matchsticks (about 1½ by ⅛ inch)
1½ cups Dashi (dried fish and kelp stock, page 20) or Kombu
    Dashi (kelp stock, page 23)
3 tablespoons mirin (sweet rice wine)
3 tablespoons Japanese soy sauce
2 teaspoons granulated sugar

Soak the *hijiki* in plenty of cold water for 30 minutes. Drain, rinse under running water, and drain well.

Heat the oil in a medium pot over medium heat. Add the carrot and cook, stirring, for 1 minute. Add the *hijiki* and cook, stirring, for 30 seconds.

Add the dashi, increase the heat to medium-high, and let it come to a strong simmer. Add the mirin, soy sauce, and sugar. Cook, uncovered, stirring occasionally, until there's no liquid left in the pot, 25 to 30 minutes. Transfer the *hijiki* to a bowl and let cool to room temperature.

Hijiki tastes best at least several hours after it's been cooked. Covered, it keeps up to 3 days in the fridge.

Note: Hijiki is sold dried and must be soaked in water before using—it expands dramatically when reconstituted, so use a big bowl. I recommend me hijiki, the leaf of the plant, which is softer and has a milder flavor that many people prefer to that of naga hijiki, or "long hijiki," which is the stem of the plant. Look for both varieties at Asian markets and health-food stores.

KAREI RAISU

Japanese curry is like the final whisper in an international game of telephone. It began in India, moved to and morphed in England, and settled in my home country, where today curry shops abound. Of course, once we adopted curry, we tweaked it endlessly to our tastes and a new dish was born. Every prefecture and every family has its own version—in Kumamoto, the meat of choice is horse. In some households, leftovers are served not with rice but with slick, chubby udon noodles. But I still love the classic combination of beef, potato, and carrot cooked in a saucy, slightly sweet curry and ladled next to white rice. You can use whatever meat and vegetables you want, but for me, curry has two unbreakable rules: First, make sure that meat is nice and fatty. Second, embrace the premade blocks of Japanese curry roux. Curry is not health food, but neither are the deep-fried pork cutlets called tonkatsu, *and I'm not planning to give those up either, no matter what my wife says!*

SERVES 4

4 tablespoons unsalted butter
2 tablespoons vegetable oil
1 large yellow onion, thinly sliced into half-moons
1 pound boneless fatty beef (such as chuck, short rib, or belly),
    cut into ¾-inch pieces
½ pound carrots (about 2 medium), peeled and roughly
    chopped into irregular ¾-inch pieces
½ pound russet potato (about 1 small), peeled and roughly
    chopped into irregular ¾-inch pieces
5 ounces medium-hot Vermont Curry (7 pieces; see Welcome
    to Vermont, next page)
1 teaspoon kosher salt
6 cups cooked short-grain white rice (page 33), hot

Heat the butter and oil in a medium pot over medium-high heat until the butter melts and bubbles. Add the onion and cook, stirring occasionally, until it's translucent and slightly wilted, about 5 minutes. Add the beef and cook, stirring occasionally, just until the pieces are no longer pink on the outside, about 5 minutes.

Add the carrots and potato, stir well, and add 7 cups of water. Bring the water to a boil over high heat, skim off any froth that appears on the surface, then reduce the heat to maintain a strong simmer. Cook, stirring occasionally, until the beef is very tender, about 1 hour. Add the curry paste and salt and continue cooking, stirring and scraping the bottom frequently, for 15 minutes more. To store, cool to room temperature and keep in an airtight container in the fridge for up to 3 days.

Divide the rice among shallow bowls, spoon on the curry, and serve immediately.

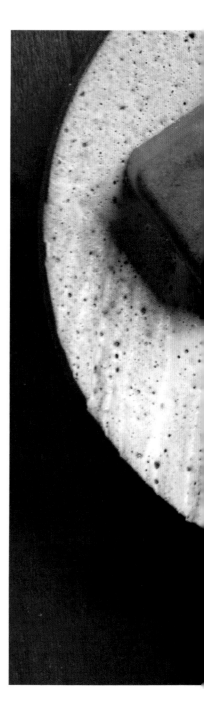

WELCOME TO VERMONT

For my curry, I recommend using a highly traditional boxed product called Vermont Curry. Yes, you read that right. You've probably seen boxes of Vermont Curry in Asian markets and wondered, "What the heck are these doing here?" Well, they're there because the seasoning blocks make delicious curry! The ingredient list makes for intriguing reading—banana and apple paste, honey, fenugreek, cheese!—but pay no attention to the slightly scary photo on the box. Your curry will look much better.

ODEN

JAPANESE-STYLE HOT POT

The French have their pot-au-feu, *the simple, celebrated stew of beef and vegetables. The Japanese have oden, a hot pot that cooks in a quarter of the time as its French counterpart but is twice the fun. Instead of endless simmering, we use the quick kelp-fueled dashi to provide the broth's backbone of flavor. And instead of plain old beef, we use hot dogs and bacon! If you think seaweed and hot dogs sound like strange bedfellows, you're about to learn that in Japan hot dogs go with anything.*

SERVES 4

4 large eggs, whole
2 small tomatoes (about ½ pound)
10 cups Dashi (dried fish and kelp stock, page 20) or Kombu
    Dashi (kelp stock, page 23)
½ pound cocktail wieners (or 2 hot dogs, quartered crosswise)
6 ounces slab bacon, cut into 1½ by ½-inch pieces
1 pound white cabbage, trimmed and cut into 4 wedges
1 large carrot, peeled and cut into 2 by ¾-inch pieces
6 very small potatoes (about ½ pound), preferably a mix of
    colors, halved if larger than 1 inch
4 medium (1-inch) Tokyo turnips
¾ ounce kombu (dried kelp), gently wiped with a damp towel
2 tablespoons *usukuchi* (Japanese light-colored soy sauce)
Kosher salt
About ¼ cup Sesame Aioli (recipe follows)
About 2 tablespoons Japanese hot mustard, or more to taste

Bring a medium pot of water to a boil. Carefully add the eggs, set a timer, and cook for 10 minutes. Transfer the eggs to a big bowl of very cold water. Add the tomatoes to the boiling water, wait about 10 seconds, then transfer them to the bowl of water. Peel the eggs and the tomatoes and set them aside.

Combine the dashi, eggs, hot dogs, bacon, cabbage, carrot, potatoes, turnips, and kombu in a wide medium pot. Bring the dashi to a boil over high heat, then reduce the heat to maintain a simmer. Cook for 10 minutes, add the soy sauce and continue cooking until the carrot is tender with a slight bite, about 5 minutes.

Halve the tomatoes, cut out the cores, and add the tomatoes to the pot. Continue cooking just until the carrot and potatoes are fully tender, about 10 minutes more. Season to taste with salt. Divide among shallow bowls and serve immediately with the aioli and mustard.

Sesame Aioli

MAKES ABOUT 1 CUP

1 large egg yolk
1 tablespoon unseasoned rice vinegar, plus more to taste
1 medium garlic clove, finely grated
½ teaspoon kosher salt, plus more to taste
¾ cup canola oil
¼ cup toasted sesame oil
Toasted sesame seeds for garnish

Whisk together the egg yolk, vinegar, garlic, and ½ teaspoon salt in a medium bowl. Put a damp kitchen towel under the bowl to steady it. Start whisking vigorously and adding the canola oil a few drops at a time, then in a minute or so, add it in a thin stream. Once you've used it up, add the sesame oil in the same way. Season to taste with vinegar and salt.

ITAME RU

To stir-fry 炒める

Japanese cooks grill, broil, fry, and steam much more often than we stir-fry. In China, on the other hand, where the cooking technique originated, there is a vast array of stir-fried dishes, too many to count. And all you need to do them justice at home is a wok, a stovetop burner with the power of a flamethrower, and several years of practice. The good news is that no recipe in the modest collection of Japanese stir-fries requires any of those things. Instead, your task is simple. Use a pan wide enough so the ingredients don't crowd (then you'd be half steaming, half stir-frying). Use high heat, though again, you do not need any pyrotechnics. And finally, as you cook, constantly stir and flip the ingredients in the pan. You don't need a flashy tossing technique: as long as the ingredients are moving around constantly (to prevent scorching), you're stir-frying!

KINPIRA

STIR-FRIED PARSNIP AND CARROT

This is Japanese home cooking at its finest. Modest root vegetables become a soulful, satisfying dish in minutes. The key is the simple seasoning whose components exist in just the right ratio. Most Japanese cooks make kinpira *with* gobo *(earthy burdock root) and* renkon *(lotus root, crisp like water chestnuts). But parsnip, carrots, and celery are easier to get and offer a similar crunch.*

SERVES 4

½ pound parsnips (about 2 large), peeled, top and bottom trimmed
¼ pound carrot (about 1 medium), peeled, top and bottom trimmed
¼ pound celery stalk (about 1 large), peeled, top and bottom trimmed
2 tablespoons toasted sesame oil
2 tablespoons mirin (sweet rice wine)
2 tablespoons Japanese soy sauce
1 teaspoon granulated sugar
A generous pinch toasted sesame seeds
A generous pinch *ichimi togarashi* (Japanese chile powder)

Quarter the parsnips, carrot, and celery lengthwise. Working with one piece at a time, lay the vegetable cut side down and thinly slice crosswise (about ⅛ inch thick) on the diagonal to get 1- to 2-inch-long pieces. Repeat with all of the vegetables. You will have about 3 lightly packed cups of parsnips, 1 lightly packed cup of carrot, and 1 lightly packed cup of celery.

Heat a large skillet over medium heat, add the sesame oil, and when it begins to smoke, add the vegetables. Cook, stirring frequently, until the vegetables begin to wilt, 2 to 3 minutes. Add the mirin and cook, stirring, for 30 seconds or so, then add the soy sauce. Cook, stirring, for 2 minutes more, then stir in the sugar.

Continue cooking, stirring frequently and reducing the heat if the vegetables threaten to color, until the vegetables are tender with a slight bite and just begin to stick to the skillet, 2 to 3 minutes.

Transfer the mixture to a bowl and sprinkle on the sesame seeds and chile powder. You can eat the *kinpira* right away, but it tastes even better left at room temperature for an hour or two. *Kinpira* can be kept refrigerated in an airtight container for up to 3 days.

YASAI ITAME

STIR-FRIED VEGETABLES

Every Japanese mama-san has a version of this simple stir-fry in her repertoire. Inspired by springtime, it celebrates the sweetness of snap peas, asparagus, and spring onions, with just enough subtle seasonings to highlight the flavors of the vegetables. A little butter adds some welcome, if nontraditional, richness.

SERVES 4

2 tablespoons *usukuchi* (Japanese light-colored soy sauce)
2 tablespoons sake (Japanese rice wine)
1 teaspoon finely grated garlic
½ teaspoon kosher salt
Ground white pepper to taste
3 spring onions (bulbs about 1 inch in diameter), roots trimmed and outer layer discarded
3 baby bok choy, trimmed and quartered lengthwise
2 cups sugar snap peas, strings removed
16 asparagus spears, tough bottoms snapped off, cut into 2-inch pieces
1 cup thin batons peeled carrot
3 tablespoons vegetable oil
2 cups roughly chopped green cabbage
½ pound *shimeji* or oyster mushrooms, trimmed and separated
1 teaspoon unsalted butter

Combine the soy sauce, sake, garlic, salt, and pepper in a small bowl, stir to dissolve the salt, and set aside.

Bring a medium pot of water to a boil. Trim all but 2 inches of the spring onion stalks. Halve the bulbs lengthwise. Add the spring onions, bok choy, snap peas, asparagus, and carrot to the water, cook for 1 minute, and drain.

Heat the oil in a large skillet over medium-high heat until it shimmers. Add the cabbage and mushrooms and cook, stirring frequently, until the cabbage wilts slightly and starts to brown in spots, 2 to 3 minutes. Add the spring onions, bok choy, snap peas, asparagus, and carrot and cook, stirring, until crisp-tender, about 2 minutes.

Add the soy sauce mixture and the butter and cook, stirring, just until the liquid has evaporated, 30 seconds to 1 minute. Serve.

KAISEN YAKI UDON

STIR-FRIED UDON NOODLES WITH SEAFOOD

Technically, there is no recipe for yaki udon, *because the components of this dish of stir-fried noodles depend on what's in your fridge. The mixture of vegetables and seafood, then, is up to you. Just follow my instructions for the sauce and make the effort to find the fat, slippery udon noodles that make the stir-fry such a pleasure to slurp. If using homemade udon noodles, boil, shock in ice water, and drain well, as instructed on page 192. Toss them with a splash of vegetable oil if you boil them for more than 5 minutes before stir-frying.*

SERVES 4

½ cup chicken stock or water
½ cup Japanese soy sauce
¼ cup oyster sauce
¼ cup sake (Japanese rice wine)
2 tablespoons granulated sugar
2 tablespoons toasted sesame oil
Black pepper to taste
1 cup sliced (¼-inch-thick bite-size) carrots
4 lightly packed cups stemmed, chopped (bite-size pieces)
   curly kale
1½ cups trimmed, halved snow peas
2 pounds fresh or frozen precooked udon noodles
3 tablespoons vegetable oil
2 cups stemmed, thinly sliced shiitake mushrooms
8 scallions, trimmed and cut into 1-inch pieces
2 cups mixed raw seafood (about 1 pound total), such as sliced
   squid, halved shrimp, and shucked mussels

Combine the chicken stock, soy sauce, oyster sauce, sake, sugar, sesame oil, and black pepper in a medium bowl and mix well.

Bring a large pot of water to a boil. Add the carrots, kale, and snow peas and cook for 2 minutes. Use a strainer to remove them from the water (keeping the water boiling) and rinse well under cold water. Gently squeeze the kale to remove excess water. Cook the udon noodles in the boiling water, stirring occasionally, just until the noodle clumps separate, about 2 minutes for fresh and 4 minutes for frozen. Drain well.

Heat the vegetable oil in a wide shallow pot or Dutch oven over medium-high heat until it shimmers. Add the mushrooms and scallions and cook, stirring occasionally, until the mushrooms start to wilt, about 2 minutes. Add the kale, snow peas, and seafood and cook, stirring occasionally, until the seafood is almost cooked through, about 2 minutes. Increase the heat to high, add the sauce, and bring to a boil. Add the noodles and cook, stirring, until the sauce thickens slightly and the noodles are well coated, about 2 minutes.

Divide among 4 plates and serve right away.

YAKISOBA

STIR-FRIED NOODLES WITH PORK, CABBAGE, AND GINGER

The most popular person at any Japanese street festival is the yakisoba *guy. Standing at a small cart with a hot griddle, he wears a twisted hair band and holds two giant spatulas, one in each hand. With great energy and fanfare he stir-fries a heap of vegetables and pork with* chukasoba *noodles—the yellow, springy Chinese-style wheat noodles more commonly known as ramen. He finishes with a glug of the special bottled sauce that tastes like a spicier version of* tonkatsu *sauce, and customers walk toward him like zombies.*

At home, however, the dish is best cooked one portion at a time. At Japanese grocery stores, chukasoba *are sold in the refrigerated section in bags with sauce packets, and labeled "yakisoba." I typically ignore the packets and instead use the tastier Otafuku brand yakisoba sauce. Why don't I make my own? Well, then the stir-fry would be a chore (you wouldn't make your own ketchup for a burger, would you?) rather than a quick lunch or perfect late-night snack.*

SERVES 1

2 tablespoons vegetable oil

2 ounces pork belly, thinly sliced, then cut into ¾-inch pieces

½ cup thinly sliced yellow onion

¼ cup 2-inch-long matchsticks peeled carrot

1 cup roughly chopped (about 2 by ¾-inch pieces) loosely packed white cabbage

One 5½-ounce package *yakisoba* noodles (a heaping cup)

2 tablespoons jarred *yakisoba* sauce, preferably the Otafuku brand

1 tablespoon shredded *beni shoga* (red pickled ginger)

1 heaping tablespoon bonito flakes

½ teaspoon *aonori* (powdered seaweed) or finely chopped nori seaweed sheets

Heat the oil in a medium-wide nonstick or cast-iron skillet over high heat until the oil shimmers. Add the pork belly, onion, and carrot and cook, stirring frequently, for about 30 seconds. Add the cabbage and cook, stirring, until it wilts slightly and the onion is lightly browned at the edges, about 3 minutes.

Add the noodles and cook, tossing with tongs, until the noodles are heated through, about 3 minutes. As you toss, gently separate the strands. (If the noodles don't separate easily, add a splash of water to the pan.) Add the sauce and continue to cook, tossing, until thoroughly coated, about 1 minute. Season with more sauce to taste, toss well, and transfer to a bowl. Top with the *beni shoga,* bonito flakes, and *aonori.* Eat right away.

MEN

Noodles 麺

Of all the noodle-cooking countries on earth, Japan is king—and I'm not biased, not at all. In this book, you'll find recipes for chubby, chewy udon noodles and thin, earthy soba (buckwheat) noodles. Why no ramen? Because the wheat noodles are almost exclusively restaurant food, not home cooking.

Even with only two types of noodle, the variations are endless, so I decided to limit my recipes to a manageable amount: one recipe for chilled udon and one for chilled soba, one for hot soba and one for hot udon. (And as a bonus, a special, highly traditional dish: spaghetti teriyaki.) Because once you learn the basics, you can invent your own versions. Cold noodles often come with a dipping sauce, the most basic version of which is simply a mixture of dashi, soy sauce, and mirin (sweet rice wine). Once you understand how to cook, rinse, and chill the noodles and make the sauce, you're ready to explore the garnishes that distinguish *ikura soba* (noodles topped with *ikura,* or salmon roe) from *oroshi soba* (noodles topped with *oroshi,* or grated daikon). Noodles served in broth

follow a similar formula: there's dashi seasoned with soy sauce and mirin, the noodles, and the ingredients that join the noodles, whether that's duck breast or fish cakes, mushrooms or tempura.

For soba, which require an expert hand to make well, my best advice is to buy them in their dried form. But while you can find fresh, tasty precooked udon noodles in many markets, I urge you to try your hand at my homemade version (page 189), which is even easier to make than fresh pasta and doesn't require a machine.

When you sit down to eat noodles, whether in your own home or at a soba restaurant, remember that Japanese table manners, unlike American manners, encourage slurping as loudly as possible. It's polite, a sign that you're enjoying what you're slurping. The extra air is said to enhance the flavor. Plus, it's fun.

KINOKO ZARU SOBA

CHILLED SOBA NOODLES WITH MUSHROOMS

Chilled soba noodles are hearty and refreshing, the perfect lunch. All that the buckwheat noodles need is a dipping sauce—just dashi, soy sauce, and mirin—and a few garnishes. Here, I stick mostly to the classic version, souping up the sauce a little by briefly steeping mushrooms in the liquid so it takes on their earthy flavor and even more umami. I love the shape and texture of beech mushrooms (known as shimeji in many markets and stores, Japanese and not), but thinly sliced shiitake or oyster mushrooms are great too.

SERVES 4

10 ounces *shimeji* (beech) mushrooms, separated, trimmed, and halved crosswise
1¼ cups Dashi (dried fish and kelp stock, page 20) or Kombu Dashi (kelp stock, page 23)
¼ cup Japanese soy sauce
¼ cup mirin (sweet rice wine)
¾ pound daikon radish, peeled and finely grated
¾ pound dried soba noodles
¼ cup thinly sliced scallion greens
¼ cup lightly packed *kizame* (shredded) nori, or 1 nori seaweed sheet, cut into thin strips with scissors

Combine the mushrooms, dashi, soy sauce, and mirin in a small saucepan and bring to a boil. Turn off the heat and let the mushrooms cool in the liquid. Transfer to a container and chill in the fridge, at least 1 hour or up to 2 days.

Put the grated radish in a pile on two layers of cheesecloth or a clean kitchen towel. Gather the edges around the radish, twist the top of the pouch, and firmly squeeze to remove excess water. Set the radish aside.

Bring a large pot of water to a boil. Cook the soba in the boiling water according to the package instructions until fully cooked but not mushy, about 4 minutes. Drain, rinse under cold water, and drain very well.

Divide among 4 bowls. Use a slotted spoon to divide the mushrooms among the bowls. Top with the radish, scallions, and nori. Serve the sauce in smaller bowls alongside for dipping or pour it over each bowl.

JAPANESE GRANDMOTHER WISDOM

When you grate daikon, keep in mind that the fatter top portion of the radish tends to be significantly sweeter and less bitter than the narrower bottom portion. Japanese cooks typically save the milder top for salads and use the more pungent bottom for grating. In this dish, the bitterness is a welcome flavor that balances the sweetness of the sauce and makes the whole thing even more refreshing.

KAMO NANBAN SOBA

You can't beat soba noodles in hot broth—wait, never mind, you can! Buckwheat noodles in salty-sweet-seasoned dashi gets even better when you add scallions, spring vegetables, and rosy red slices of duck. Arrange the slices in the soup at the last minute so they finish cooking and leak a little fat into the broth.

SERVES 4

¾ pound boneless duck breast (1 medium or 2 small), silver skin removed if necessary
Kosher salt and black pepper
8 cups Dashi (dried fish and kelp stock, page 20) or Kombu Dashi (kelp stock, page 23)
¾ cup Japanese soy sauce
¾ cup mirin (sweet rice wine)
16 medium asparagus spears, tough bottoms snapped off, cut into 1½-inch pieces
1 cup fiddlehead ferns or trimmed, halved sugar snap peas
8 scallions, trimmed and cut into 1½-inch pieces
¾ pound dried soba noodles
½ teaspoon toasted sesame seeds

Bring a large pot of water to a boil.

Put the duck skin side up on a cutting board. Use a sharp knife to score the skin all over (cutting through the fat but not into the meat) in a crisscross pattern. Season both sides with salt and pepper.

Heat a medium skillet over medium heat until it's hot. Add the duck skin side down and cook until the skin is golden brown and some of the fat has rendered, about 8 minutes. Turn over the breast and cook just until the underside is golden brown, about 4 minutes. The duck will still be slightly rare inside. Let rest for 5 minutes, then thinly slice the duck crosswise and set aside.

Combine the dashi, soy sauce, and mirin in a medium pot and bring to a boil. Add the asparagus, fiddlehead ferns, and scallions to the boiling water and cook just until they're cooked through but still have bite, about 2 minutes. Use a strainer to scoop them into the pot with the dashi (keep the water boiling). Add the sliced duck to the pot with the dashi and turn off the heat. The duck will finish cooking with the residual heat.

Cook the soba in the boiling water according to the package instructions until fully cooked but not mushy, about 4 minutes. Drain very well and divide among 4 bowls. Distribute the vegetables, duck, and broth among the bowls and top each with the sesame seeds.

HOMEMADE UDON NOODLES

Dried udon noodles are fine. Store-bought precooked udon work well. But there's nothing like homemade udon, and believe it or not, you really can make the irresistibly slick, chewy, springy noodles at home. Udon take no great skill. Just flour, water, a rolling pin, and a little patience. If kneading the dough, which activates the gluten in the flour and gives the noodles their texture, makes your arms tired, do what home cooks in Japan do: put the dough in a resealable plastic bag, wrap it in a towel, and knead with your feet!

MAKES 2 POUNDS (4 PORTIONS)

Special equipment
Rolling pin

600 grams all-purpose flour (about 5 cups), sifted through a
    strainer, plus more for dusting and tossing
1 tablespoon plus 1 teaspoon kosher salt
1¼ to 1½ cups water

MAKE THE DOUGH

Combine the flour and salt in a large mixing bowl, stir, then add 1¼ cups of the water. Use your hands to mix until the dough starts to come together in a few large lumps. Start to firmly press and knead the dough, incorporating the loose flour until there's none left. If necessary, add a little more water, 1 tablespoon at a time, until you can incorporate all of the flour.

Lightly dust a work surface with flour, add the dough, and knead (folding and firmly pressing with your palm, folding and pressing) until the dough looks and feels fairly smooth, about 5 minutes. Form the dough into a ball, wrap it in plastic wrap, and let it rest at room temperature for 1 hour.

On a lightly floured surface with ample room, knead it again for about 2 minutes. Lightly dust both sides with flour, then use the rolling pin to roll

(Recipe continues on page 192)

(Continued from page 189)

the dough, occasionally rotating the dough 90 degrees and lightly dusting with flour if it threatens to stick to the pin, into a rough, approximately 17-inch circle with an even thickness (slightly less than ¼ inch). If you are having difficulty rolling, allow the dough to rest for 5 to 10 minutes as needed. This allows the glutens to relax and make it easier to roll out.

Fold the dough into thirds, then slice widthwise into approximately ⅛-inch-thick noodles. Gently separate the noodles and toss them with a little bit of flour, just so they don't stick together. Cook right away.

TO COOK HOMEMADE UDON

The way you cook homemade noodles is slightly different from the way you cook purchased noodles. Follow these instructions whether you're planning to serve the noodles hot or cold.

Bring a large pot of water to a boil and prepare a large bowl of icy water. Add the noodles to the boiling water, stirring frequently and adding ¼ cup of fresh water if the water threatens to bubble over, until they're fully cooked but not mushy, 10 to 12 minutes. (Unlike Italian pasta, they shouldn't be al dente, but don't let them get mushy.)

Drain them, then transfer them to the icy water. Briefly and gently rub them with your hands to remove some of the starch. Drain very well.

ZARU UDON

Udon noodles are so deliciously chewy that enjoying them requires nothing more than this simple, classic preparation: a dipping sauce, a few fun toppings, and a pair of chopsticks to help you slurp them up. The louder, the better. This dish is best when made with homemade udon noodles that have been boiled, shocked in ice water, and drained well, as instructed on page 192.

SERVES 4

1½ cups Dashi (dried fish and kelp stock, page 20) or Kombu
    Dashi (kelp stock, page 23)
¼ cup plus 2 tablespoons Japanese soy sauce
¼ cup plus 2 tablespoons mirin (sweet rice wine)
2 pounds Homemade Udon Noodles (page 189), or fresh or
    frozen precooked udon noodles
¼ cup lightly packed *kizame* (shredded) nori, or 1 nori seaweed
    sheet, cut into very thin strips
¼ cup toasted sesame seeds
¼ cup thinly sliced scallion greens
1 generous tablespoon finely grated ginger

Combine the dashi, soy sauce, and mirin in a large, wide pot and bring to a boil over high heat. Let the mixture cool, transfer to a container, and chill in the fridge, at least 1 hour or up to 3 days.

Bring a large pot of water to a boil. Add the udon noodles and cook according to the package instructions until fully cooked but not mushy, about 3 minutes for fresh and 5 minutes for frozen. Drain, rinse under cold water, and drain very well.

Divide the noodles among 4 bowls and top with the nori. Serve the sauce in smaller bowls alongside for dipping or pour it over each bowl. Serve the sesame seeds, scallions, and ginger alongside so everyone can top his or her own bowl.

NABEYAKI UDON

"CLAY POT" UDON NOODLE SOUP

When I feel November's first frigid wind, my first thought is, "Maybe it's time to check on my restaurant in Hawaii." If I can't, I know I'll be okay—after all, there's always nabeyaki udon. *Traditionally served in an earthenware hot pot called a* donabe *that retains heat really well, the soup is the ultimate cold-weather comfort food. Each portion is a meal, thanks to slick, springy udon noodles, chicken, greens, and the strange but wonderful pink-rimmed fish cake called* kamaboko. *Another classic addition is shrimp tempura, plunked right into the soup to soak up the luscious, egg-enriched broth. For a real treat, use homemade udon noodles that have been boiled, shocked in ice water, and drained well, as instructed on pages 192.*

SERVES 4

6 cups Dashi (dried fish and kelp stock, page 20) or Kombu
    Dashi (kelp stock, page 23)
½ cup mirin (sweet rice wine)
½ cup *usukuchi* (Japanese light-colored soy sauce)
2 pounds Homemade Udon Noodles (page 189), or fresh or
    frozen precooked udon noodles
¼ pound boneless chicken thighs, cut into thin bite-size pieces
Eight ¼-inch-thick half-moon slices *kamaboko* (Japanese fish
    cake)
4 medium fresh or rehydrated (page 254) dried shiitake
    mushroom caps
4 cups very loosely packed baby spinach, dunked in boiling
    water, then squeezed well
4 cups very loosely packed stemmed *shungiku* (chrysanthemum
    greens), or more baby spinach
2 scallions, whites and light green parts, cut into 2 by ½-inch
    strips
4 large eggs
4 pieces shrimp tempura (page 207)
Shichimi togarashi (Japanese seven-spice powder) to taste

Combine the dashi, mirin, and soy sauce in a wide, shallow pot and bring to a boil over high heat. Add the udon noodles and cook, stirring occasionally, just until the noodle clumps separate, about 2 minutes for fresh noodles and 4 minutes for frozen noodles.

Add the chicken, fish cake, and mushrooms onto the noodles, each ingredient in its own cluster. Reduce the heat to maintain a strong simmer if necessary. Cook, without stirring but turning over the chicken pieces once, until the chicken is cooked through, about 3 minutes. Reduce the heat slightly. Add the spinach, chrysanthemum greens, and scallions onto the noodles, each in its own cluster. Cook just until the greens begin to wilt and the noodles are fully cooked but not mushy, about 1 minute. Add each egg to a different area of the pot, taking care not to break the yolks. Cover the pot and cook until the egg whites have just set and the noodles are fully cooked but not mushy, about 3 minutes. Add the shrimp tempura so it floats on the surface.

Bring the pot to the table along with 4 large bowls and a small dish of the *shichimi togarashi* for sprinkling.

SUPAGETTI NO TERIYAKI

CHICKEN TERIYAKI SPAGHETTI

You might not be surprised to hear that Japanese people love noodles, but you might not expect that our affection for ramen, soba, and udon is nearly matched by our fondness for spaghetti. And since Japanese cooks have for a long time gone their own way with the Italian pasta—tossing it with ketchup or finishing it with butter and spicy fish roe—I don't think they'll sneer at my creation. Spaghetti takes the place of rice, which is the more typical accompaniment to chicken teriyaki, and gives you a reason to enjoy even more of the beloved sweet-salty sauce.

SERVES 4

2 pounds boneless chicken thighs, breasts, or a mixture
¾ pound dried spaghetti
Kosher salt
2 tablespoons vegetable oil
1 cup teriyaki sauce (page 108)
1 tablespoon cornstarch
About 8 large basil leaves, torn at the last minute

If you're using chicken breasts, place a breast between two sheets of plastic wrap and pound it out to an even ½-inch thickness. Repeat with the remaining breasts.

Cook the pasta in a large pot of generously salted boiling water according to the package instructions until al dente. Drain well.

Meanwhile, lightly season both sides of the chicken with salt. Heat the oil in a large skillet over high heat until it shimmers. Cook the chicken in two batches to avoid crowding the skillet until deep golden brown on one side, about 6 minutes. Flip the chicken, reduce the heat to medium, and cook until just cooked through, 4 to 5 minutes more. Transfer the chicken to a cutting board as it's cooked. Let it rest a few minutes, then cut it against the grain into bite-size slices.

Combine the chicken and teriyaki sauce in a large skillet and bring the sauce to a simmer over medium-high heat. In a small container,

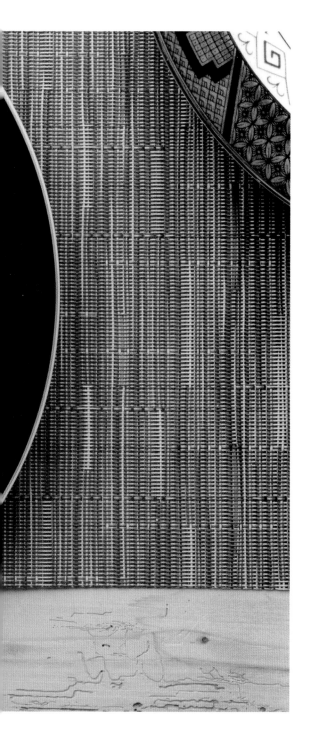

stir together the cornstarch and 1 tablespoon water until smooth. Drizzle in the cornstarch mixture, stirring constantly. Let the mixture return to a simmer and cook until the sauce has thickened slightly, about 1 minute. Add the pasta and cook, tossing frequently, until the sauce coats the noodles well, about 1 minute. Sprinkle on the basil and serve right away.

AGERU

To fry 揚げる

Many people think sushi is to thank for the Japanese food boom in America. Me? I blame tempura. Before Americans embraced raw fish, they were eagerly eating lightly battered vegetables made enticing from a dip in bubbling oil. Because what foods aren't improved by crunch? As if attempting to answer the question, in Japan, we deep-fry everything: Pork cutlets? Sure. Tofu? Absolutely. Fish-cake-wrapped hot dogs? Of course! We've also elevated the cooking method into an art form. At the hushed temples to tempura in Tokyo, customers hand over hundreds for seasonal vegetables and pristine sea creatures fried to order by masters of hot oil.

Despite our love of frying, it is a relatively new import to the Japanese kitchen, brought to the country by Portuguese traders in the sixteenth century. Our love of deep-frying today is just more evidence of the Japanese talent for adopting delicious foreign foods and making them even better.

I know that when many home cooks hear the word *fry,* they want to hide under the sink. So I want to address two misconceptions that keep people from creating crunchy treats at home. First, many cooks assume that it's impossible to do at home without an electric deep fryer and 911 on speed dial. In fact, all you need is a sturdy pot and a deep-fry (or candy) thermometer, an inexpensive device that clips to the side of the pot. To be safe, just use your noodle—don't drop items into the oil, place them. And keep liquids like water away from the oil.

The second big misconception is that frying is horrible for your health. After all, you're using so much oil! *Aha,* but if you follow my instructions, you'll be frying with oil at the right temperature, which means barely any of the fat will soak into the batter. As you fry, do your best to maintain this temperature, which will dip whenever ingredients are added, by adjusting the heat underneath the pot.

SAVE YOUR OIL

Even though very little of it ends up in your food, deep-frying does require a lot of oil. Here's a tip: Don't dump the oil after you cook. Instead, strain it through a fine-mesh sieve and reserve it for your next deep-frying adventure.

YASAI TEMPURA

VEGETABLE TEMPURA

Tempura is not about hiding vegetables. It's about celebrating them! In fact, the better the tempura, the less batter you see. So use the best vegetables you can find—I like to call them "sushi-quality" vegetables—and focus on the batter. The keys to success are ice water and a very light hand when mixing in the flour. Both prevent the gluten in the flour from activating, which keeps the coating delicate and less likely to suck up oil when it fries. To help further, I recommend using tempura batter mix rather than the old school mixture of cake flour and eggs. It's much more forgiving.

SERVES 4

Special Equipment
Deep-fry (or candy) thermometer

Vegetable oil for deep-frying (about 12 cups)
Salt
18 green beans, ends trimmed
3 small Japanese eggplants, quartered lengthwise
Eight ¼-inch-thick round slices unpeeled Japanese sweet
  potato (*satsuma imo*)
Ten ¼-inch-thick unpeeled half-moon slices small kabocha
  squash

For the Batter
2 cups purchased tempura batter mix, plus about ½ cup for
  coating
2 cups cold water

For Serving
Tempura sauce, curry salt, and/or matcha salt (see Dunking
  and Dipping, page 206)

Preheat the oven to 200°F. Line a baking sheet with a wire rack or with brown paper bags. Pour about 3 inches of vegetable oil into a medium pot and set it over medium-high heat until the oil reaches 350°F on the deep-fry thermometer.

DUNKING AND DIPPING

Unlike many Western fried foods, tempura isn't seasoned with salt—not before it's fried or after. The salty component comes in the form of condiments. At the finest tempura restaurants, these often take the form of infused salts. At more modest ones, sauce does the trick, served along with grated daikon and ginger that you mix in to taste. I provide recipes for all three, though I encourage you to go wild. I've been known to dunk my tempura in Argentinean chimichurri sauce and even ranch dressing.

TEMPURA SAUCE: Combine 1 cup Dashi (dried fish and kelp stock, page 20), ¼ cup mirin, and ¼ cup Japanese soy sauce in a small pot, bring to a boil, and let cool to room temperature.

CURRY SALT: Stir together 1 tablespoon kosher salt and 1 teaspoon Madras curry powder.

MATCHA SALT: Stir together 1 tablespoon kosher salt and ½ teaspoon matcha powder.

Meanwhile, bring a small pot of water to a boil and season it lightly with salt. Add the green beans and cook until crisp-tender, about 2 minutes. Drain and run under cold running water until cool to the touch. Drain well and pat dry.

Sift the 2 cups of tempura batter mix into a medium mixing bowl. (You can use a sifter or add the flour to a sieve and tap the edge of the sieve against your palm so the flour falls through the holes.) Add a few ice cubes to the cold water and stir vigorously to chill. Strain the water into the tempura batter mix and use chopsticks or the handle of a long spoon (not a whisk) to gently stir until the flour and water are not quite combined (you should still see a little raw flour at the sides of the bowl) and very lumpy. Put the remaining ½ cup tempura batter mix on a medium plate and spread it out slightly.

Just before you fry, stir the oil well. Cook one type of vegetable at a time. Add a few pieces to the plate of tempura batter mix and toss briefly to just barely coat them in a very thin layer of flour. Shake off any excess flour, submerge the pieces briefly in the batter, and carefully add them to the oil.

Fry, adjusting the heat if necessary to maintain the oil temperature and turning the pieces over occasionally, until they're crunchy but before they're colored, 2 to 3 minutes. Scoop out the excess fried bits, return the oil temperature to 350°F, and repeat with the remaining vegetables of that type. Transfer them to the prepared baking sheet and keep warm in the oven while you fry the remaining vegetables in the same way.

Serve hot with tempura sauce, curry salt, and/or matcha salt (see Dunking and Dipping, opposite).

SHRIMP TEMPURA

As much as I love to eat a parade of tempura vegetables, I get especially excited when I see that shrimp has joined the party. Ocean sweet and tender beneath its crunchy exterior, the deep-fried crustacean makes a welcome addition to the plate, to bowls of Nabeyaki Udon (page 195), or in deliciously inauthentic hand rolls (page 53) along with spicy mayo and butter lettuce. They make a particularly striking addition, because they appear long and stick-straight. But wait, you might wonder, aren't shrimp curled? Here's the secret:

Remove the shell except for the final segment at the tail. Remove the vein from the back of each shrimp. Turn them over so that backs are against the cutting board (curve facing up) and make five shallow (about ¼ inch) crosswise cuts—about one every ½ inch—on the bottom of each one. Firmly bend the shrimp to fully straighten them, pat them dry, and lay them flat on a cutting board.

Toss 12 jumbo shrimp (about ¾ pound), with ¼ cup dry tempura batter mix. Sift 1 cup of tempura batter mix into a medium bowl. Stir a few ice cubes into 1 cup cold water and then strain the water into the bowl. Batter and fry just like the vegetable tempura, for 2 to 3 minutes.

KAKI AGE

SHRIMP AND VEGETABLE FRITTERS

If you crossed tempura with latkes, you'd get these airy, crunchy clusters of shrimp and vegetables. These fritters are easy to form with a spoon, as instructed in the recipe, but for a particularly neat shape, look to a noodle strainer. To form each one, add about ½ cup of the shrimp mixture to the strainer basket, press gently, then lower the basket into the oil.

SERVES 4

Special Equipment
Deep-fry (or candy) thermometer

Vegetable oil for deep-frying (about 8 cups)
½ pound medium shrimp, peeled, deveined, and cut crosswise
    into 4 pieces
½ small yellow onion, cut with the grain into thin half-moon
    slices and separated
1½ cups loosely packed very roughly chopped mitsuba or
    julienned celery
1 cup peeled burdock root (*gobo*) or parsnip matchsticks (3 by
    ⅛ inch)
¾ teaspoon kosher salt
¾ cup purchased tempura batter mix
½ cup cold water
Tempura sauce, curry salt, and/or matcha salt for serving (see
    Dunking and Dipping, page 206)

Pour 2 to 3 inches of vegetable oil into a wide shallow pot and set it over medium-high heat until the oil reaches 350°F on the deep-fry thermometer.

Meanwhile, combine the shrimp, onion, mitsuba, burdock root, salt, and ¼ cup of the tempura batter mix in a medium mixing bowl. Toss well.

Put the remaining ½ cup tempura batter mix in a small bowl. Add a few ice cubes to the water and stir vigorously. Strain the water into the bowl with the tempura batter mix and use chopsticks or the handle of a long spoon (not a whisk) to gently stir until the flour and water are not quite combined

(you should still see a little raw flour at the sides of the bowl) and very lumpy. Pour the tempura batter into the bowl with the shrimp mixture and toss briefly but well.

Fry the *kaki age* in two batches of four. Carefully spoon approximately ½-cup mounds of the shrimp mixture into the oil and fry, turning each over after 1 minute, until the onion is light golden, the *kaki age* are crispy, and the shrimp turn pink, 3 to 4 minutes.

Transfer them to paper towels or a cooling rack to drain. Return the oil to 350°F and fry the remaining *kaki age* in the same way. Serve immediately.

KARA AGE

JAPANESE-STYLE FRIED CHICKEN WITH SCALLION SAUCE

I've eaten fried chicken all over the world, so I can say with confidence that Japan's version competes with the very best out there. Briefly marinated in ginger, garlic, and soy sauce and coated in cornstarch instead of the typical flour, the chicken leaves the hot oil juicy, flavorful, and, unlike the typical heavily battered bird, surprisingly light. Because you're not dealing with big, bone-in pieces, the frying is quick and painless.

SERVES 4

Special Equipment
Deep-fry (or candy) thermometer

For the Sauce
3 tablespoons Japanese soy sauce
2 tablespoons unseasoned rice vinegar
1 tablespoon mirin (sweet rice wine)
1 tablespoon granulated sugar
1 teaspoon toasted sesame oil
3 tablespoons thinly sliced scallions
4 fresh shiso leaves (also called Japanese mint and perilla),
    finely chopped

For the Chicken
2 large eggs, lightly beaten
1 cup plus 2 tablespoons cornstarch
2 tablespoons sake (Japanese rice wine)
1 tablespoon plus 1 teaspoon Japanese soy sauce
2 teaspoons granulated sugar
1 teaspoon finely grated garlic
1 teaspoon finely grated ginger
½ teaspoon kosher salt
1½ pounds boneless, skinless chicken thighs, cut into 2-inch
    pieces
Vegetable oil for deep-frying (about 8 cups)

MAKE THE SAUCE

Combine the soy sauce, vinegar, mirin, sugar, and sesame oil in a small bowl and stir until the sugar dissolves. Just before you serve, stir in the scallions and shiso.

MAKE THE CHICKEN

Combine the eggs, 2 tablespoons of the cornstarch, the sake, soy sauce, sugar, garlic, ginger, and salt in a large mixing bowl and stir until the sugar dissolves. Add the chicken, toss well, and set aside to marinate for at least 15 minutes or covered in the fridge for up to a few hours.

Pour 2 to 3 inches of vegetable oil in a medium pot and set it over medium-high heat until the oil reaches 350°F on the deep-fry thermometer.

Put the remaining 1 cup of cornstarch in a large mixing bowl. Lift half of the chicken out of the marinade, letting the excess drip off. Add it to the cornstarch and toss to thoroughly coat each piece. Do not shake off the excess cornstarch. Use tongs to add the chicken pieces one by one to the oil and fry, stirring and flipping the chicken occasionally, until it's crispy and the visible meat is golden brown, about 6 minutes. Transfer them to paper towels or a cooling rack to drain. Repeat with the remaining chicken.

Serve immediately with the dipping sauce alongside.

JAPANESE GRANDMOTHER WISDOM

Daikon are slightly larger than your typical salad radish. In fact, some daikon have been known to weigh more than a small child. The specimens you'll spot will probably be closer to a pound or so, which means you'll occasionally find yourself with extra. Wondering what to do with it? Finely grate it and use it to make fried chicken even more tender and delicious: toss about ½ cup of finely grated daikon with the raw chicken you plan to use for *kara age*, and let it sit for a couple of hours. Wipe off the daikon before proceeding with the recipe.

TONKATSU

JAPANESE-STYLE FRIED PORK CUTLET

Japanese cooks love to take Western dishes and make them their own. That's how tonkatsu—essentially, breaded pork cutlets—became one of the most beloved foods in my home country. In the typical Japanese fashion, affection has developed into obsession, with restaurants dedicated to tonkatsu *and chefs debating over the proper cuts of pork, the type of fat (pork lard? sesame oil?), and frying temperature. Yet at home, serving* tonkatsu *is as simple as making chicken cutlets but ten times as delicious thanks to extra-crunchy panko breadcrumbs and umami-packed* tonkatsu *sauce.*

SERVES 4

Special Equipment
Deep-fry (or candy) thermometer

For the Cutlets
Vegetable oil for deep-frying (about 10 cups)
Four ½-inch-thick pork loin cutlets (about 1 pound total),
    preferably with fat cap attached
Kosher salt and ground white pepper
About 1½ cups panko breadcrumbs
About 1 cup all-purpose flour
2 large eggs, beaten

For Serving
3 cups very thinly sliced white cabbage
Lemon wedges
Tonkatsu Sauce (recipe follows)

Pour about 2 inches of vegetable oil into a medium pot and set it over medium-high heat until the oil reaches 350°F on the deep-fry thermometer.

Use the tip of a sharp knife to score the cutlets, making about a dozen short, shallow cuts all over each side. This keeps the cutlets from curling as they fry. Season both sides lightly with salt and pepper.

Put the panko, flour, and eggs in three separate wide bowls. Working with one cutlet at a time, add it to the flour and turn to coat it, shaking off any excess. Transfer it to the egg and turn to coat, letting any excess egg drip off. Finally, transfer it to the panko, turning to coat well and piling on some of the panko and pressing lightly with your hands. The goal is to get as much panko to adhere as you can. Transfer the breaded cutlet to a plate and repeat with the remaining cutlets. Discard any leftover flour, egg, and panko.

Soak the cabbage in icy water for 10 minutes and drain well.

Just before you fry, stir the oil well. Fry the cutlets two at a time, adjusting the heat if necessary to maintain the oil temperature and turning the pieces over occasionally, until the cutlets are golden brown and crispy, 5 to 6 minutes. Transfer to paper towels to drain and fry the remaining cutlets. Let the cutlets rest for a few minutes, then cut them into ¾-inch slices and serve with the cabbage, lemon, and sauce for dipping.

Tonkatsu Sauce

I can't bring myself to say you can't use one of the many bottled versions of this sweet-tangy sauce. After all, even homemade versions rely on other bottled products. Yet making it yourself lets you control the sweetness. I leave my version chunky, but feel free to blend if you prefer a smoother sauce.

MAKES ABOUT ¾ CUP

¼ cup toasted sesame seeds
½ cup seeded, cored, finely chopped canned whole tomatoes
3 tablespoons Worcestershire sauce
3 tablespoons ketchup
2 tablespoons molasses (not blackstrap)
1 teaspoon garlic powder
⅛ teaspoon kosher salt, or to taste

Put the sesame seeds in a medium pan, set it over medium heat, and toast, stirring and tossing frequently, until they're a few shades darker, about 3 minutes. Transfer them to a bowl and let them cool.

Combine the remaining ingredients in a small saucepan, stir, and set over medium heat. Bring the sauce to a simmer, lower the heat to maintain a gentle simmer, and cook, stirring occasionally, until the flavors come together, about 10 minutes. Season to taste. Transfer the sauce to a bowl and let it come to room temperature. It keeps in the fridge for up to 1 week.

When you're ready to serve, pound the seeds to a powder in a mortar or grind them in a spice grinder and serve in a bowl at the table, instructing your guests to mix the paste into the sauce to taste.

MENCHI KATSU

CRISPY FRIED BEEF PATTIES

Like their cousin tonkatsu, *these croquettes mix the pleasures of Japanese cuisine with those of the American South. No culture, it seems, can resist the allure of fried meat. My take on the dish is nothing more than* hambagu *patties, breaded and submerged into oil until the outsides are crispy and brown and the insides practically burst with juiciness.*

SERVES 4

Special Equipment
Deep-fry (or candy) thermometer

For the Patties
1 tablespoon unsalted butter
1 medium yellow onion, very finely diced
½ cup panko breadcrumbs
¼ cup plus 2 tablespoons whole milk
1 pound ground beef (80% lean)
1 teaspoon kosher salt
½ teaspoon grated nutmeg
White pepper to taste
1 large egg
1 tablespoon vegetable oil for your hands

For Frying
Vegetable oil for deep-frying (about 8 cups)
About 2 cups panko breadcrumbs
About 1 cup all-purpose flour
2 large eggs, beaten
Tonkatsu Sauce (page 217)

MAKE THE PATTIES

Heat a medium skillet over medium-high heat, add the butter, and let it melt. Add the onion and cook, stirring frequently, until the onion is translucent and light brown at the edges, 10 to 15 minutes. Let the onion cool. Meanwhile, combine the panko and milk in a medium bowl, stir to moisten the crumbs, and let the mixture sit for 5 minutes or so.

Add the onion, beef, salt, nutmeg, and white pepper to the bowl with the panko mixture and mix firmly with your hands until the ingredients are well distributed and the mixture is slightly sticky to the touch, about 1 minute. Add the egg and mix again, about 30 seconds more.

Using lightly oiled hands, grab about a quarter of the meat mixture and firmly toss it back and forth between your hands for about 1 minute, or 30 seconds if you're quick. (The goal—unlike that of most Western hamburger makers—is to get rid of most of the air hiding out in the patties.) Form 4 patties of more or less equal size (about 4½ inches in diameter and ½ inch thick).

BREAD AND FRY THE PATTIES

Pour about 1½ inches of vegetable oil into a wide shallow pot and set it over medium-high heat until the oil reaches 365°F on the deep-fry thermometer.

Put the panko, flour, and eggs in three separate wide bowls. Working with one patty at a time, add it to the flour and turn to coat it, shaking off any excess. Transfer it to the egg and turn to coat, letting any excess egg drip off. Finally, transfer it to the panko, turning to coat well and piling on some of the panko and pressing lightly with your hands. The goal is to get as much panko to adhere as you can. Transfer the patty to a plate and repeat with the remaining patties. Discard any leftover flour, egg, and panko.

Just before you fry, stir the oil well. Fry the patties two at a time, adjusting the heat if necessary to maintain the oil temperature and turning the pieces over occasionally, until the cutlets are deep golden brown and crispy, 5 to 6 minutes. Transfer to paper towels to drain and fry the remaining patties.

Let the patties rest for a few minutes, then serve with *tonkatsu* sauce on the side.

KABOCHA KOROKKE

SQUASH CROQUETTES

These crunchy croquettes wouldn't seem out of place at a dinner party in Tennessee, yet they're straight out of the Japanese grandmother's playbook. The classic filling is a mixture of mashed potato and ground meat, but I swap out the meat for squash, because I love the earthy sweetness and cool orange color.

SERVES 4

Special Equipment
Deep-fry (or candy) thermometer

¾ pound peeled, seeded kabocha squash (about ½ medium squash), cut into 4 equal-size pieces
¾ pound russet potato, peeled and quartered lengthwise
½ cup frozen corn kernels, defrosted and drained well
1 teaspoon kosher salt
Vegetable oil for deep-frying (about 8 cups), plus extra for your hands
About 2 cups panko breadcrumbs
About 1 cup all-purpose flour
2 large eggs, beaten
Tonkatsu Sauce (page 217)

Put a steamer insert in a large pot with a lid (or use a colander as long as the lid can still close). Add about ½ inch water to the pot, cover, and bring to a boil over high heat. Steam the squash and potato until they're fully tender but not mushy, about 15 minutes.

Coarsely mash them in a bowl and let cool. Stir in the corn and salt.

Pour about 2 inches of vegetable oil into a medium pot and set it over medium-high heat until the oil reaches 375°F on the deep-fry thermometer.

Meanwhile, put the panko, flour, and eggs in three separate wide bowls. Rub a little oil on your hands. Form the squash mixture into eight 3 by 1-inch croquettes. Working one at a time, add a croquette to the flour and turn to coat it, shaking off any excess. Transfer it to the eggs and turn to coat, letting any excess egg drip off. Finally, transfer it to the panko, turning to coat well while piling on some of the panko and pressing lightly with your hands. Transfer to a plate and repeat with the remaining croquettes, discarding any leftover flour, egg, and panko.

Just before you fry, stir the oil well. Fry in a few batches, adjusting the heat if necessary to maintain the oil temperature and gently stirring occasionally, until the croquettes are golden brown and crispy, 2 to 3 minutes per batch. Transfer to paper towels to drain and fry the rest.

Serve immediately with the *tonkatsu* sauce for dipping.

AE RU

To dress 和える

When I say "Japanese salad," you probably picture iceberg lettuce and slivers of carrot doused in ginger dressing. In this chapter, however, I would like to redefine the word *salad* so it can encompass Japan's enticing but little known roster of room-temperature, vegetable-focused dishes tossed in oil-free sauces. These, my friends, fall into the category of *ae mono*—roughly translated as "dressed things." Whether the sauce in question is made from sesame seeds (as in *goma ae*) or tofu (as in *shira ae*), these dishes offer a great opportunity to show off seasonal goodies or spruce up vegetables in your fridge. *Ae mono* are often served in small portions, to be eaten with several other dishes, perhaps rice, soup, and grilled fish. Yet when I want to be particularly healthy, I'll up the portion size and scale back on the rice.

INGEN NO GOMA AE

GREEN BEANS WITH SESAME DRESSING

Freshly toasted sesame seeds spiked with soy sauce and mirin become a nutty, rich dressing for crunchy green beans. This dish is great at room temperature: remember this recipe the next time you are planning a picnic or packing a bento-box lunch.

SERVES 4

3 tablespoons toasted sesame seeds
About 1 tablespoon kosher salt
2 cups trimmed, halved green beans
1 tablespoon Japanese soy sauce
1 tablespoon mirin (sweet rice wine)
1 teaspoon granulated sugar

Put the sesame seeds in a small skillet, set it over medium heat, and toast, stirring and tossing frequently, until they're a few shades darker, 2 to 3 minutes. Transfer them to a bowl to cool. Pound the seeds in a mortar or buzz in a spice grinder until you have a slightly coarse powder.

Bring a small pot of water to a boil and season it with salt as if you're seasoning soup. Prepare a bowl of icy water. Add the green beans to the pot and cook, stirring occasionally, until they're fully cooked but still have a slight crunch, about 3 minutes. Drain the beans, immediately transfer them to the icy water, and stir well. When the green beans are cool, drain and pat them dry.

Combine the soy sauce, mirin, sugar, and sesame powder in a medium mixing bowl and stir until combined. Add the green beans and stir to coat them well. Mound the green beans on a plate and serve. The beans can be kept refrigerated in an airtight container for up to a day.

KARASHI AE

Standard renditions of karashi ae *rely on boiled or steamed vegetables, but in the colder months, when Brussels sprouts and maitake mushrooms (also called hen of the woods) are in season, I break with tradition and roast them in the oven. Shrimp adds substance, turning this into a hearty side dish. Karashi means "mustard," so expect a dish that nips at your nose. Dashi, however, tones down the bite and ups the umami, leaving a subtle dressing that lets the vegetables shine.*

SERVES 4

2½ tablespoons vegetable oil
½ pound medium shrimp, peeled and deveined
1½ teaspoons kosher salt, plus more for seasoning
½ pound Brussels sprouts, trimmed and quartered through
   the stem
6 ounces fresh maitake mushrooms or oyster mushrooms, cut
   into bite-size pieces
1¼ cups Dashi (dried fish and kelp stock, page 20) or Kombu
   Dashi (kelp stock, page 23)
1 tablespoon plus 1 teaspoon Japanese soy sauce
1 tablespoon plus 1 teaspoon mirin (sweet rice wine)
1 to 2 tablespoons Japanese hot mustard, or more to taste

Preheat the oven to 425°F.

Heat 1 tablespoon of the oil in a large ovenproof skillet over medium-high heat until it shimmers. Lightly season the shrimp with salt and cook, flipping once, until they're lightly browned on both sides and just cooked through, about 3 minutes. Transfer the shrimp to a cutting board and cut crosswise into 3 or 4 pieces and set aside.

Add the remaining 1½ tablespoons vegetable oil to the skillet, add the Brussels sprouts and mushrooms, and toss well. Cook, stirring occasionally, for 2 minutes, then transfer the skillet to the oven. Cook, stirring once, until the Brussels sprouts are tender with a slight bite and lightly browned, 8 to 10 minutes. Let cool slightly.

Meanwhile, combine the dashi, soy sauce, mirin, and 1½ teaspoons salt in a medium pot, set it over medium heat, and stir just until the salt dissolves. Let the mixture cool and stir in 1 tablespoon of the mustard. Season to taste with more salt and mustard.

Add the Brussels sprouts, mushrooms, and shrimp to the dashi mixture, toss well, and transfer to a large shallow bowl or divide among small bowls. Eat right away.

SHIRA AE

Take a quick glance at shira ae *and you'd be forgiven for thinking it was boring
health food. Yet the coarse white dressing isn't cottage cheese—it's tofu perked up
with soy sauce and mirin. And the vegetables aren't raw—they're steeped in dashi
to infuse them with flavor. It's still health food, though, just far from boring.*

SERVES 4

Special Equipment
Cheesecloth

4 cups loosely packed trimmed spinach (not baby)
4 medium dried shiitake mushroom caps, rehydrated (page
   254) and thinly sliced
½ cup carrot matchsticks (about 1½ by ⅛ inch)
1½ cups Dashi (dried fish and kelp stock, page 20) or Kombu
   Dashi (kelp stock, page 23)
1½ tablespoons plus about 1 teaspoon mirin (sweet rice wine)
2 teaspoons plus about 1 teaspoon Japanese soy sauce
Generous pinch kosher salt
One 14-ounce package firm tofu, drained

Bring a small pot of water to a boil. Prepare a bowl of icy water. Add the
spinach to the boiling water, stir well, and cook for 20 seconds. Use a
slotted spoon or spider to transfer the spinach to the icy water. Stir well,
drain, firmly squeeze the spinach to remove as much water as you can, and
set aside.

Combine the shiitake, carrots, dashi, 1½ tablespoons mirin, 2 teaspoons
soy sauce, and the salt in a small pot and bring to a boil over high heat.
Reduce the heat to maintain a simmer and cook for 10 minutes, so the dashi
flavor begins to infuse the vegetables. Take the pot off the heat and let cool
slightly. Add the spinach, stir well to loosen the clumps, and let the mixture
sit at room temperature for at least 30 minutes or up to 2 hours.

Set the tofu on two layers of cheesecloth, gather the edges of the cheesecloth around the tofu, and squeeze firmly over the sink to extract as much water as possible. Add the tofu to a medium mixing bowl and crumble it with your fingers.

Drain the vegetables, squeeze them gently to remove some of the liquid they've absorbed, and add them to the bowl along with the remaining soy sauce and mirin (or a little more to taste). Toss well, breaking up any tofu chunks larger than ¼ inch. Eat right away or store in an airtight container in the fridge for up to a day. Let it come to room temperature before eating.

JAPANESE GRANDMOTHER WISDOM

Grandmothers aren't fussy cooks—they just have good taste. So when they blanch spinach for dishes like *shira ae* or *ohitashi,* they use this simple trick to make sure the dense stems are fully cooked before the delicate leaves overcook. They line up the stems and leaves, grab the spinach by the leaves, and lower the stems into boiling water for 15 seconds before adding the whole handful to the water. This way, the stems get the head start they need.

SUMISO AE

SQUID AND SCALLIONS
WITH MISO-VINEGAR DRESSING

Headlining the dressing for sumiso ae *are the brightness of rice vinegar and the famous fermented soybean paste that's Japan's greatest contribution to planet Earth since Kurosawa and karate. Here, the mixture works its magic on squid, though the same amount of chicken thigh or breast, cut into thin strips and blanched until just cooked through, works well too. As you follow the recipe, keep your eyes peeled for a cool trick that gives you especially sweet scallions, taking them from garnish to show stealer.*

SERVES 4

For the Sauce
2 tablespoons *aka* (red) miso
2 tablespoons granulated sugar
2 tablespoons sake (Japanese rice wine)
1 tablespoon unseasoned rice vinegar
1 teaspoon mirin (sweet rice wine)
1 teaspoon Japanese soy sauce
½ teaspoon Japanese hot mustard

For the Dish
Kosher salt
4 bunches scallions, roots and top 2 inches trimmed
½ pound cleaned squid, bodies cut into ½-inch-thick rings,
    legs cut into bite-size pieces
1 teaspoon toasted sesame seeds

MAKE THE SAUCE

Bring an inch or two of water to a boil in a small pot. Stir together the miso, sugar, and sake in a medium heatproof bowl that will fit snugly in the pot without making contact with the boiling water. Set the bowl over the pot and let the heat from the boiling water gently cook the mixture, stirring and scraping the sides of the bowl occasionally, until it has thickened slightly and the color has turned a shade darker, 12 to 15 minutes. Let the mixture cool.

Combine the miso mixture with the vinegar, mirin, soy sauce, and mustard and stir until very smooth. The sauce keeps in an airtight container in the fridge for up to 3 days.

MAKE THE DISH

Bring a medium pot of lightly salted water to a boil. Add the scallions and cook, prodding to keep them more or less submerged, until the whites are tender (they should give slightly when you squeeze them), about 2 minutes. Transfer them to a cutting board and let them cool slightly. Add the squid to the boiling water and cook until it's just cooked through, 30 seconds to 1 minute. Drain well and let it cool.

Line up the scallions on the cutting board so the white ends face the same direction. Working with 4 or 5 scallions at a time, use one hand to steady the whites. Using the side of your other hand or the back of a knife, apply slight pressure to the whites and move toward the tip of the greens, forcing out as much of the water from inside the scallions as possible. Then, steady the greens and use the side of your hand to force the water out of the white ends. Discard the liquid and cut the scallions into 1-inch lengths.

Combine the squid, scallions, and sauce in a mixing bowl, toss well, and divide among 4 plates. Sprinkle with the sesame seeds and serve.

TSUKERU

To pickle

漬ける

If pickling makes you fret about sterilization techniques and cupboards full of Ball jars, think again. Modern Japanese pickling is a different animal, more about transformation than preservation—perfect for today's cooks, who no longer need to make cucumbers last through the winter and who rarely have a glut of carrots to put up. And what a transformation it is! Using a few different methods, such as brining and simple fermentation but not typically soaking in vinegar, Japan cooks make humble vegetables into lively, crunchy delights. Instead of weeks, the pickles in this chapter take just twenty-four hours to mature. That means it's easy to eat the Japanese way, with pickles alongside every meal to refresh your palate.

TATAKI KYURI

SMASHED CUCUMBER PICKLES

Hi-yah! *Smashing cucumbers with a slap of your knife is fun and a great way to blow off steam. It's also a great way to jump-start pickling, breaking down the vegetable so the brine can penetrate more quickly. A last-minute toss in sesame seeds and soy sauce makes a fine pickle even finer.*

MAKES ABOUT 3 CUPS

1 pound crunchy, narrow cucumbers, such as Japanese,
    Persian, or Kirby
1 tablespoon plus 1 teaspoon kosher salt
1 ounce (about 2 inches) peeled ginger, very thinly sliced
⅓ ounce kombu (dried kelp), an approximately 3-inch square
2 Asian small dried red chiles, halved, seeds discarded
3 tablespoons sesame seeds
1 tablespoon Japanese soy sauce

Halve the cucumbers lengthwise and scoop out the seeds. Cut the cucumbers into approximately 2-inch lengths. Use the side of the blade of a chef's knife to firmly slap each piece so it's well bruised but stays in one or two pieces.

Combine the salt and 4 cups of water in a large container with an airtight lid and stir until the salt dissolves. Add the ginger, kombu, chiles, and cucumbers and stir well.

Cover the container with plastic wrap, pressing it against the surface of the vegetables (this helps keep them submerged). Cover with the lid and refrigerate for at least 24 hours or up to 3 days.

When you're ready to eat, put the sesame seeds in a small skillet, set it over medium heat, and toast, stirring and tossing frequently, until they're a few shades darker, 3 to 5 minutes. Transfer them to a bowl to cool. Pound the seeds in a mortar or buzz in a spice grinder until you have a slightly coarse powder. Combine the powder in a bowl with the soy sauce and stir well.

Use a clean slotted spoon to scoop out the cucumber and add it to the bowl with the sesame seed mixture. Toss well and serve.

SHIOZUKE

SALT PICKLES

Perhaps the simplest pickles in the Japanese repertoire, shiozuke are briefly brined in a simple salt-and-water solution with a little kombu thrown in to boost the umami quotient. This makes cabbage and radish—though cucumber and carrot work great too—tender but still crunchy, salty but still full of natural sweetness. In other words, even more fun to eat.

MAKES ABOUT 3 CUPS

- 2 tablespoons kosher salt
- ⅓ ounce kombu (dried kelp)
- 2 Asian dried red chiles or 1 fresh jalapeño, halved, seeds discarded
- ½ pound trimmed red radishes (about 8), cut into ¼-inch-thick round slices
- ½ pound white cabbage leaves (about 8), roughly torn into 2- or 3-inch pieces

Combine the salt and 4 cups of water in a large container with an airtight lid and stir until the salt dissolves. Add the kombu, chile, radishes, and cabbage and stir well.

Cover the container with plastic wrap and press the plastic wrap against the surface of the vegetables (this helps keep them submerged). Cover with the lid and refrigerate for at least 24 hours or up to 3 days.

When you're ready to eat, use a clean slotted spoon to scoop out as much cabbage and radish as you'd like. Transfer it to a kitchen towel, squeeze firmly to remove excess water, and eat.

MISOZUKE

The sweet-salty flavor of miso works its way into vegetables, making some seriously addictive pickles. In Japan, carrots and turnips, cucumbers and daikon all end up submerged in miso, but here, asparagus and bell pepper make colorful alternatives.

Once your pickles are ready, you'll have lots of leftover miso mixture. Don't throw it out! Stir in a generous ¼ cup more miso and use for the mixture for a second batch of miso pickles.

MAKES ABOUT 3 CUPS

1 pound *shiro* (white) miso (about 2 cups)
½ cup plus 2 tablespoons sake (Japanese rice wine)
½ cup plus 2 tablespoons mirin (sweet rice wine)
¼ cup plus 2 tablespoons granulated sugar
½ pound asparagus, tough bottoms removed, stalks peeled
3 medium red, yellow, and/or green bell peppers, stemmed, seeded, and cut into 3 by 1-inch pieces

Put the miso in a large mixing bowl. Combine the sake, mirin, and sugar in a small pot and cook, stirring, over medium heat just until the sugar dissolves, about 2 minutes. A quarter at a time, pour the hot mixture into the bowl with the miso, stirring well after each addition. You should have a relatively smooth paste.

Add the vegetables to the miso paste, stir well, and transfer to airtight containers, making sure that the vegetables are covered with a layer of the paste. Cover and keep refrigerated for 24 hours.

Remove the vegetables, reserving the paste. Rinse the vegetables and pat them dry. You can keep them in airtight containers for up to 3 more days or slice and eat right away.

NUKAZUKE

RICE BRAN PICKLES

Did you know that white rice is really just brown rice without its jacket? That jacket is rice bran, sold for cheap in health-food stores and Japanese supermarkets and used in Japan to make irresistible pickles. You bury vegetables—anything from cucumber and eggplant to parsnips and burdock root to kohlrabi or turnip—in a mixture of salt, water, and rice bran, and in just a day or so, they've transformed through the magic of fermentation into crunchy, earthy, tangy treats.

Traditionally, every family had a crock at home to make nukazuke. *Every day they'd pull vegetables from the rice bran mixture and replenish the mixture with more rice bran. Like sourdough starter, this mixture has been in some families for years, even decades.*

MAKES ABOUT 4 CUPS

½ pound Japanese or narrow Italian eggplant
½ pound crunchy, narrow cucumbers, such as Japanese, Persian, or Kirby
½ pound carrots, peeled and halved lengthwise if thicker than 1 inch
½ cup plus 2 tablespoons kosher salt
2 pounds rice bran (*nuka;* see Bread and Beer Pickles, opposite)
1 ounce kombu (dried kelp), very coarsely crumbled
6 Asian dried red chiles, halved and seeded

Using the tip of a sharp knife, make about 6 long, shallow lengthwise slits just through the skin of the eggplant. Briefly run the eggplant, cucumbers, and carrots under water, then use your hands to rub them with 2 tablespoons of the salt. Let them sit for 15 minutes.

Meanwhile, combine the rice bran, kombu, chiles, and remaining ½ cup salt in a large bowl and stir well. Add 3 cups water and use a spoon or gloved hands (*nuka* makes some people's hands itch) to stir until the mixture looks like wet sand.

Without rinsing or drying the vegetables, add them to the rice bran mixture. Make sure they're covered on all sides by the rice bran mixture, including a thick layer on top. Cover the bowl with plastic wrap and keep in a cool, dry place for at least 24 hours or up to 2 days. (Alternatively, keep the bowl in the refrigerator for 3 days.)

Remove the vegetables, reserving the rice bran mixture for your next batch of pickles. You can keep them in airtight containers for up to one more day. When you're ready to eat, rinse, pat dry, and slice them into bite-size pieces.

BREAD AND BEER PICKLES

If you can't get your hands on rice bran, substitute 2 pounds of panko breadcrumbs and 3 cups of light-colored beer instead of water. The mixture mimics the flavor of rice bran and makes an excellent, if slightly more mild, pickle.

Acknowledgments

A big, heartfelt thank-you to everyone who helped make this book possible.

To everyone at Ecco, especially Dan Halpern, Gabriella Doob, and Suet Chong.

To my amazing agent, Kimberly Witherspoon, and her team at Inkwell.

To Chiaki Takada, Misaki Harada, Takao Iinuma, and Ariki Omae for their tireless work.

To the entire Morimoto restaurant family for all your hard work to make me look good.

To JJ Goode for keeping this project moving and helping to make it great.

To Evan Sung for his incredible photography.

To Andrea Albin for her careful recipe testing.

To Oyama-san for hiring and teaching me.

To my mother for her love and for teaching me how not to cook.

To my wife, who is a better cook than I am.

Ingredient Glossary

BURDOCK ROOT

This long, thin, brown-skinned root vegetable, called *gobo* in Japanese, is prized for its nutty, earthy flavor and crisp texture. Look for fresh burdock root, preferably no more than 1 inch thick, at Asian markets as well as some farmers' markets and supermarkets. Avoid frozen or canned. Burdock root will turn brown when exposed to air, so keep it submerged in water to prevent discoloration until you're ready to cook (but no more than 15 minutes). Parsnip makes an acceptable substitute.

DAIKON RADISH

This large white radish is juicy and crisp with a strong, peppery flavor. It can be eaten raw, but is often simmered, pickled, and steamed. Look for those that are heavy for their size and without wrinkles or cracks. Daikon radish is available at Japanese and Asian markets as well as many supermarkets and farmers' markets.

DRIED BONITO FLAKES

The tuna-like fish called bonito (or *katsuo* in Japanese) is smoked, dried, then cured to make *katsuobushi,* an umami-rich pantry staple and one of the prime ingredients in dashi stock. When I was a kid, cooks shaved *katsuobushi* into feathery flakes using a special box with a blade and a small drawer to collect the shavings. Today, most home cooks use preshaved flakes.

Look for bonito flakes in bags at Japanese and Asian markets, as well as some health-food stores and online. If you see multiple brands, which is uncommon in the United States, use price as an indicator of quality. Store unopened packets in a cool, dry spot, away from light. Once opened, store bonito flakes, tightly sealed, in the refrigerator and use within three weeks.

DRIED SHIITAKE

With their concentrated flavor and long shelf life, dried shiitakes are a Japanese pantry staple. Look for them at Asian and American supermarkets. Buy whole dried mushrooms (ignore slices) and look for thick caps, which are more expensive but have better flavor and texture.

To rehydrate dried shiitake: Soak the mushrooms in warm water, laying a damp kitchen towel over the surface of the water if necessary to keep them submerged, until they're fully tender, about 30 minutes for thick-capped mushrooms. Drain them, reserving the soaking liquid to use as a flavorful cooking liquid. Gently squeeze the mushrooms to remove excess water and cut off the tough stems.

DUMPLING WRAPPERS

In Japanese markets, you'll see wrappers labeled "gyoza" and "shumai," so it's easy to tell which to buy when you're making Gyoza (pork and cabbage dumplings, page 109) or Shumai (Japanese-style shrimp dumplings, page 125). Yet non-Japanese Asian markets and even some American supermarkets sell dumpling wrappers that work well for making Japanese dumplings. For either type, look for round, white-colored (also known as "Shanghai style") wrappers in the refrigerated section, typically near the fresh noodles.

ICHIMI TOGARASHI

Not to be confused with *shichimi togarashi* (a mixture of moderately hot chile powder and other dried spices), *ichimi togarashi* contains only chile powder. Look for it at Japanese and Asian markets and some supermarkets. Keep it in a cool, dark place for up to three months.

JAPANESE MUSTARD

Made from only mustard seeds and no vinegar, Japanese mustard (*karashi*) is significantly more potent than its Western counterparts, nose-tinglingly sharp, and slightly bitter. It's sold as a powder (*konakarashi*) or paste (*nerigarashi*). The paste is just mustard powder that's been blended with water, which you can do yourself: add just enough water to form a thick paste and let the paste sit, covered, for about 5 minutes before using.

Most Japanese and Asian markets stock one or both forms of *karashi* (sometimes labeled "hot mustard" or "Japanese mustard"). If you can't find either one, look for Chinese mustard powder or use Colman's English mustard powder.

KOMBU

Kombu is a dried sea kelp that the Japanese have been harvesting and cultivating for centuries, mostly from the cold waters off Hokkaido. An essential component to dashi stock, it contains naturally occurring glutamates, the source of its much-prized umami.

Look for kombu (often labeled "dashi kombu") at Japanese and Asian markets as well as health-food stores. Kombu comes in many varieties and grades, but in the United States, it's unusual to find more than one or two on offer. If you do have options, use price as an indicator of quality. Note that the white powder on the surface of kombu is not a sign of age or poor quality but rather of those umami-producing glutamates. Do not scrub it off before using. Store dried kombu in an airtight container in a cool, dry spot away from light. Use it within a year.

Note: Some cookbooks call for an amount of kombu by its dimensions. But since kombu varies in thickness and is often curled on itself, I prefer to use weight. If you don't have an inexpensive food scale, use the weight on the package to estimate the weight of the pieces you use.

KONNYAKU CAKE

This gelatinous cake made from dried, powdered *konnyaku* (also called *konjac* or devil's tongue) has a very mild flavor, springy texture, and an incredibly low calorie content. Typically used in soups and stews, *konnyaku* cake takes on the flavor of the liquid in which it's cooked. Look for packages of *konnyaku* cake (sometimes labeled "*konjac* cake" or "yam cake") in the refrigerated section of Japanese markets as well as some Asian markets and health-food stores. The cake comes in white and gray varieties, which have a similar flavor. For this book, use the gray variety.

MIRIN

Sometimes called sweet rice wine, mirin is a slightly sweet amber-colored liquid that has about the same alcohol content as wine but less than sake. It's not technically wine, however; it's made from fermented glutinous rice and distilled alcohol. Today the most common versions have little alcohol but contain ingredients meant to mimic the flavor of true mirin. Look for true mirin at some specialty wine stores, and common mirin at Asian markets and health-food stores. Once opened, refrigerate mirin and be sure to wipe the cap and rim after each use to prevent sticking.

MISO

This salty, fermented product is a staple of the Japanese kitchen and the star of one of its most beloved dishes, miso soup. Yet miso has many uses in the Japanese kitchen, in marinades and stews, sauces and pickling beds. Miso comes in many colors and varieties. Most miso is made from soybeans and rice, though *mugi* miso is made from a mixture of soybeans and barley and *hatcho* miso is made exclusively from soybeans. Other varieties are distinguished by the color and length of fermentation.

For this book, you need to know just two varieties: *Shiro* miso (literally "white miso," but also known as "sweet miso") has the shortest fermentation time, a mellow flavor, and a relatively low salt content. *Aka* miso (literally "red miso") has been fermented longer than *shiro* miso. It has a bolder flavor and tends to be saltier. That said, different brands of miso vary in flavor and saltiness, so always season to taste with salt.

Miso is available at Japanese and Asian markets, health-food stores, and many supermarkets. Store miso in an airtight container in the refrigerator for up to a year.

MISTUBA

Sometimes called Japanese parsley or trefoil, this herb has a bright, green, mild flavor and shows up often in Japanese cooking. It can be difficult to find outside of Japanese markets. If you can't find mitsuba, try Chinese celery, parsley, or even cilantro instead.

NORI

By now every American is familiar with nori, the seaweed that wraps sushi rolls and *onigiri* (rice balls). Made from a variety of red algae that's chopped to a pulp, formed into sheets, and dried using techniques borrowed from Japanese papermaking, nori is sold as crisp green sheets (each about 8½ by 7½ inches) at Japanese and Asian markets, health-food stores, and some supermarkets. If you have a choice of brands, let price be your guide to quality.

PANKO BREADCRUMBS

These coarse Japanese breadcrumbs, made from crustless Japanese-style white bread (called *shokupan*), have an airy, flaky texture that becomes especially crisp and crunchy when deep-fried. Nowadays, many supermarkets stock panko breadcrumbs, though there's still a chance you'll need to visit a Japanese or other Asian market. Store panko breadcrumbs in an airtight container in a cool, dry spot away from light; they will keep for a couple of months.

RICE VINEGAR

Made from fermented rice and other grains, rice vinegar is mellow and fragrant, much less acidic than distilled white vinegar and many vinegars popular in the West. Avoid seasoned rice vinegar (if you're unsure, check the ingredient list), which contains sugar and salt in addition to vinegar. Rice vinegar is available at Japanese and Asian markets as well as some health-food stores and supermarkets.

SAKE

Often misleadingly called "rice wine," sake is made using a process that is closer to beer brewing than wine making. Rice is polished, steamed, treated with koji mold, and fermented with yeast. The result is a beverage that's as elegant as wine, and the finest versions fetch the same high prices. Yet sake is also a staple pantry ingredient. When buying sake for cooking, you must balance price and quality. The cheapest product is "cooking sake," which like wine sold exclusively for cooking, contains added sugar, salt, and preservatives and should be avoided. Yet you'd be crazy to heat top-quality sake. Instead, visit liquor or wine shops or licensed Japanese supermarkets and ask for inexpensive sake that's dry, not sweet. Store sake tightly capped in a cool, dry spot away from light.

SHICHIMI TOGARASHI

This mixture of dried spices contains "seven flavors" (*shichimi*), including chiles (*togarashi*) and ingredients like citrus peel, sesame seeds, and sansho pepper (similar to Sichuan peppercorn), though the specific ingredients and proportions differ by brand. Not to be confused with *ichimi togarashi* (chile powder with no other spices added), *shichimi togarashi* is available at Japanese and Asian markets and some supermarkets. Keep it in a cool, dark place for up to three months.

SHISO

Called *oba* in Japanese and sometimes labeled "Japanese mint," this herb has jagged green leaves and a unique minty, slightly peppery flavor. Look for it in Japanese markets. If you can't find green shiso, look at Southeast Asian markets for red or purple perilla (*tia to* in Vietnamese). This variety has darker green leaves with purplish undersides and a similar, though more aggressive, flavor.

SOY SAUCE

Perhaps the most iconic seasoning in the Japanese kitchen, soy sauce is made from fermented soybeans and wheat. The recipes in this book call for two types of soy sauce: the dark kind (*koikuchi shōyu*) found in every supermarket and light-colored soy sauce (*usukuchi shōyu*), which is saltier than the darker soy sauce and typically available only at Japanese or other Asian markets. To achieve the right flavor for the dishes in this book, make sure to buy Japanese soy sauce (not Chinese or Thai). If you have a chance to choose among different brands, let price be your guide to quality.

TOASTED SESAME OIL

This translucent brown oil made from toasted sesame seeds—not the yellowish one made from raw seeds—is the one to buy for Japanese cooking. Sesame oils are available at Japanese and Asian markets, health-food stores, and some supermarkets. Store sesame oil tightly capped in a cool, dark place for up to six months or in the refrigerator for slightly longer.

TOBANJAN

This spicy, salty product is often translated as "chile bean sauce." The paste comes from China, where it's used often in Sichuan cooking, but Japanese cooks use it often to contribute umami and heat. For the recipes in this book, try to find a Japanese brand such as Youki. Chinese brands are easier to find at supermarkets and Asian markets and make a good substitute.

WAKAME

This versatile and highly nutritious sea vegetable is used in soups, noodles, simmered dishes, and salads. Wakame is typically available in dried form at Japanese and Asian markets, health-food stores, and some supermarkets. Dried wakame needs to be soaked in cold water for five minutes; it will swell to its original volume and turn smooth and green.

Sources

Long ago—in the 1990s—poor access to Japanese ingredients kept Americans from making dashi, tempura, and miso-marinated fish at home. Not anymore. Today, miso is almost as easy to find as ketchup. Japanese markets are no longer the only places to find kombu, *umeboshi,* and rice vinegar—you can buy all these and more at health-food stores and even many supermarkets like Whole Foods. And perhaps the best news yet: because so many Japanese staples are preserved foods, they ship well and can be ordered from this place called the Internet. You won't believe what you can have delivered to your door, from high-quality soy sauce to fresh mitsuba, dobin teapots, and sushi-making robots! Here are a few websites that will help you stock your kitchen.

AMAZON

amazon.com

Explore this little-known website and be rewarded with a selection of rice cookers, rice wine vinegars, *yuzu kosho,* dried shiitake, dobin teapots, and virtually anything else you type into the search bar.

GOLD MINE NATURAL FOOD CO.

goldminenaturalfoods.com

A natural foods company in San Diego that will happily mail you products including high-quality mirin and dried soba noodles, *umeboshi* made by a family in Nara prefecture, and dried sea vegetables like kombu, *me hijiki,* and nori.

KATAGIRI

katagiri.com

This New York City–based Japanese grocery store will ship you ingredients such as gray *konnyaku,* fresh udon and *yakisoba* noodles, Otafuku brand *yakisoba* sauce, kombu, and *hijiki.*

KORIN

korin.com

An incredible knife shop that also sells all sorts of cool Japanese cookware, from items you'll use often (*otoshibuta, onigiri* molds, bamboo steamers) to specialty items (wooden battera molds, special pans for making *oyako* and *tamagoyaki*) to rice ball–forming "sushi robots."

MITSUWA

mitsuwa.com

Think Super Stop & Shop with the aisles filled with Japanese products— that's Mitsuwa, a giant market with locations in New Jersey, in Chicago, and several in California. Its online store sells just about everything fresh, frozen, bottled, and dried that you need to cook from this book: fresh mitsuba and mountain yam, frozen black cod and sushi-quality tuna, *ichimi* and *sichimi togarashi,* pickled red ginger, *kamaboko* fish cake, and bonito flakes. It's all here.

Index

Note: Page numbers in *italics* indicate photographs.

A

ae ru (to dress), 225

Ingen No Goma Ae (green beans with sesame dressing), 227, *228–29*

Karashi Ae (Brussels sprouts, shrimp, and mushrooms with mustard dressing), 230–31

Shira Ae (spinach, carrot, and shiitake with tofu dressing), *232*, 233–34

Sumiso Ae (squid and scallions with miso-vinegar dressing), 235–36, *237*

ageru (to fry), 201–03

Green Bean Clusters, 207

hana o sakaseru technique, 207

Kabocha Korokke (squash croquettes), *220*, 221–22

Kaki Age (shrimp and vegetable fritters), 208–09, *209*

Kara Age (Japanese-style fried chicken with scallion sauce), *210*, 211–13

Menchi Katsu (crispy fried beef patties), 218–19

Tonkatsu (Japanese-style fried pork cutlet), *214*, 215–17

Yasai Tempura (vegetable tempura), *204*, 205–07

Asari No Miso Shiru (miso soup with clams), 78, *79*

B

bamboo shoot(s)

Chikuzenni (chicken simmered with lotus root and bamboo shoot), *152*, 153–54, *154*

Battera (pressed mackerel sushi), *60*, 61–65, *62–63*

beef

Hambagu (Japanese-style hamburger with tangy sauce), 146–47, *147*

Karei Raisu (Japanese-style curry), *160*, 161–62

Menchi Katsu (crispy fried beef patties), 218–19

Nikujaga (Japanese-style beef stew), 155–56, *157*

Suteki Don (steak rice bowls with spicy teriyaki sauce), 70–71

bonito flakes (katsuobushi)

Dashi (dried fish and kelp stock), 20, *21*

Bread and Beer Pickles, 247

Brussels sprouts

Karashi Ae (Brussels sprouts, shrimp, and mushrooms with mustard dressing), 230–31

Buta No Kakuni (slow-cooked pork belly with beer-teriyaki glaze), *148–49*, 150–51

Buta No Shogayaki (pork belly with ginger and onions), 118, *119*

C

cabbage
Gyoza (pork and cabbage
dumplings), 109–12, *110–11, 113*
Yakisoba (stir-fried noodles with
pork, cabbage, and ginger), *176,*
177–78, 179
California Temaki, *58,* 59
carrots
Kinpira (stir-fried parsnip and
carrot), *170,* 171–72
Shira Ae (spinach, carrot, and
shiitake with tofu dressing), *232,*
233–34
Chahan (Japanese-style fried rice), *46,*
47–49
Chawanmushi (egg custard with
shrimp, chicken, and fish), *132,*
133–34, *135*
chicken
Chawanmushi (egg custard with
shrimp, chicken, and fish), *132,*
133–34, *135*
Chikuzenni (chicken simmered with
lotus root and bamboo shoot),
152, 153–54, *154*
Dango Jiru (Japanese-style chicken
and dumpling soup), *86,* 87–88
Kara Age (Japanese-style fried
chicken with scallion sauce),
210, 211–13
Nasu No Misoyaki (eggplant with
chicken and miso sauce), 104–05
Oyako Don (chicken and egg rice
bowl), *66,* 67–68
Supagetti No Teriyaki (chicken
teriyaki spaghetti), 197–99, *198*

Tori No Teriyaki (chicken teriyaki),
106, 107–08
Tsukune No Teriyaki (chicken
meatballs with teriyaki sauce),
98–99
Yakitori Party (grilled chicken
and vegetable skewers), *94,*
95–97
Chikuzenni (chicken simmered with
lotus root and bamboo shoot),
152, 153–54, *154*
Chirashi Zushi (scattered sushi), 52
clams
Asari No Miso Shiru (miso soup
with clams), 78, *79*
cucumbers
Tataki Kyuri (smashed cucumber
pickles), 240, *241*
curry
Karei Raisu (Japanese-style curry),
160, 161–62
using premade seasoning, 162
Curry Salt, 206

D

daikon radish, using, 185, 213
Dango Jiru (Japanese-style chicken and
dumpling soup), *86,* 87–88
Dashi (dried fish and kelp stock), 20, *21*
tips for making, 17
Dobin Mushi (aromatic "tea pot" soup
with mushrooms, fish, and
shrimp), 89–90, *91*
Donburi (rice bowls), 65
Katsu Don (pork cutlet and egg rice
bowl), *69*

Oyako Don (chicken and egg rice
  bowl), *66, 67*–68
Suteki Don (steak rice bowls with
  spicy teriyaki sauce), 70–71
Tekka Don No Poke (Hawaiian
  poke-style tuna rice bowl), *72,
  73*
duck
  Kamo Nanban Soba (soba noodle
    soup with duck and spring
    vegetables), 186–87
dumplings
  Dango Jiru (Japanese-style chicken
    and dumpling soup), *86,* 87–88
  Gyoza (pork and cabbage
    dumplings), 109–12, *110–11, 113*
  Shumai (Japanese-style shrimp
    dumplings), *124,* 125–31, *126–29*

E
eggplant
  Nasu No Misoyaki (eggplant with
    chicken and miso sauce),
    104–05
eggs
  Chawanmushi (egg custard with
    shrimp, chicken, and fish), *132,
    133–34, 135*
  Katsu Don (pork cutlet and egg rice
    bowl), 69
  Omuraisu (omelet with ketchup-
    fried rice), *40,* 40–41
  Oyako Don (chicken and egg rice
    bowl), *66, 67*–68
  Tamago Supu (Japanese egg drop
    soup), *84,* 85

Tamagoyaki (Japanese omelet),
  115–17, *116–17*

F
fish and seafood
  Asari No Miso Shiru (miso soup
    with clams), 78, *79*
  Battera (pressed mackerel sushi), *60,
    61*–65, *62–63*
  Chawanmushi (egg custard with
    shrimp, chicken, and fish), *132,
    133–34, 135*
  Dobin Mushi (aromatic "tea pot"
    soup with mushrooms, fish, and
    shrimp), 89–90, *91*
  Kaisen Yaki Udon (stir-fried udon
    noodles with seafood), 174–75
  Kaki Age (shrimp and vegetable
    fritters), 208–09, *209*
  Karashi Ae (Brussels sprouts,
    shrimp, and mushrooms with
    mustard dressing), 230–31
  Nitsuke (fish simmered with sake,
    soy sauce, and sugar), *144,* 145
  Saba No Misoni (mackerel
    simmered with miso), *140,*
    141–42
  sakajio fish seasoning technique,
    101
  Sakana No Misoyaki (grilled miso-
    marinated fish), 102–03, *103*
  Sakana No Sakamushi (fish steamed
    in kombu with spicy soy sauce),
    122, 122–23
  Sake Shioyaki (salt-grilled salmon),
    100, *101*

fish and seafood (*continued*)

    Shrimp Shells, Furikake with Potato Chips and, 34–35, *34–35*

    Shumai (Japanese-style shrimp dumplings), *124,* 125–31, *126–29*

    Sumiso Ae (squid and scallions with miso-vinegar dressing), 235–36, *237*

    Tekka Don No Poke (Hawaiian poke-style tuna rice bowl), *72,* 73

    Tuna Mayo, 38

    Tuna Temaki, Spicy, *55,* 55–56

Furikake with Shrimp Shells and Potato Chips, 34–35, *34–35*

G

ginger

    Buta No Shogayaki (pork belly with ginger and onions), 118, *119*

    Yakisoba (stir-fried noodles with pork, cabbage, and ginger), *176,* 177–78, *179*

    Zaru Udon (chilled udon noodles with scallions and ginger), 193

gohan (rice), 25–28

    Battera (pressed mackerel sushi), *60,* 61–65, *62–63*

    buying a rice cooker, 29

    California Temaki, *58,* 59

    Chahan (Japanese-style fried rice), *46,* 47–49

    Chirashi Zushi (scattered sushi), 52

    Donburi (rice bowls), 65

    Hakumai (perfect white rice), *32, 33*

    Katsu Don (pork cutlet and egg rice bowl), 69

    Omuraisu (omelet with ketchup-fried rice), *40,* 40–41

    Onigiri (rice balls), *36,* 37–38

    Oyako Don (chicken and egg rice bowl), *66,* 67–68

    Su Meshi (sushi rice), 50–52, *51*

    Suteki Don (steak rice bowls with spicy teriyaki sauce), 70–71

    Takikomi Gohan (dashi-simmered rice with vegetables), *42,* 43–44, *45*

    Tekka Don No Poke (Hawaiian poke-style tuna rice bowl), *72,* 73

    Tuna Temaki, Spicy, *55,* 55–56

    Ume-Shiso Temaki, 56

    Vegetable Temaki, *57,* 57–58

    Yaki Onigiri (grilled rice balls), 39

green beans

    Green Bean Clusters, 207

    Ingen No Goma Ae (green beans with sesame dressing), *226,* 227, *228–29*

Gyoza (pork and cabbage dumplings), 109–12, *110–11, 113*

H

Hakumai (perfect white rice), *32, 33*

Hambagu (Japanese-style hamburger with tangy sauce), 146–47, *147*

hana o sakaseru frying technique, 207

Hijiki (sweet simmered hijiki seaweed), 158, *159*

I

ichiju sansei (the Japanese meal), 10–12

Ingen No Goma Ae (green beans with sesame dressing), *226*, 227, *228–29*

itame ru (to stir-fry), 169

Kaisen Yaki Udon (stir-fried udon noodles with seafood), 174–75

Kinpira (stir-fried parsnip and carrot), *170*, 171–72

Yakisoba (stir-fried noodles with pork, cabbage, and ginger), *176*, 177–78, *179*

Yasai Itame (stir-fried vegetables), 173

itazuri salting technique, 59

K

Kabocha Korokke (squash croquettes), *220*, 221–22

Kaisen Yaki Udon (stir-fried udon noodles with seafood), 174–75

Kaki Age (shrimp and vegetable fritters), 208–09, *209*

kale

Ohitashi (dashi-marinated kale), 22

Kamo Nanban Soba (soba noodle soup with duck and spring vegetables), 186–87

Kara Age (Japanese-style fried chicken with scallion sauce), *210*, 211–13

Karashi Ae (Brussels sprouts, shrimp, and mushrooms with Japanese mustard dressing), 230–31

Karei Raisu (Japanese-style curry), *160*, 161–62

Katsu Don (pork cutlet and egg rice bowl), 69

katsuobushi (bonito flakes)

Dashi (dried fish and kelp stock), 20, *21*

Kinoko Zaru Soba (chilled soba noodles with mushrooms), 184–85

Kinpira (stir-fried parsnip and carrot), *170*, 171–72

kombu (kelp), 16

Dashi (dried fish and kelp stock), 20, *21*

Sakana No Sakamushi (fish steamed in kombu with spicy soy sauce), *122*, 122–23

Kombu Dashi (kelp stock), 23

L

lotus root

Chikuzenni (chicken simmered with lotus root and bamboo shoot), *152*, 153–54, *154*

M

mackerel

Battera (pressed mackerel sushi), *60*, 61–65, *62–63*

Saba No Misoni (mackerel simmered with miso), *140*, 141–42

Matcha Salt, 206

meat, slicing, 119

men (noodles), 181–83. *See also* noodle stir-fries

men (noodles; *continued*)

Homemade Udon Noodles, *188,*
189–92, 190–91

Kamo Nanban Soba (soba noodle
soup with duck and spring
vegetables), 186–87

Kinoko Zaru Soba (chilled soba
noodles with mushrooms),
184–85

Nabeyaki Udon ("clay pot" udon
noodle soup), *194,* 195–96

Supagetti No Teriyaki (chicken
teriyaki spaghetti), 197–99, *198*

Zaru Udon (chilled udon noodles
with scallions and ginger), 193

Menchi Katsu (crispy fried beef
patties), 218–19

miso

Asari No Miso Shiru (miso soup
with clams), 78, *79*

Miso Shiru (miso soup with tofu),
76, 77

Misozuke (miso pickles), 243

Nasu No Misoyaki (eggplant with
chicken and miso sauce), 104–05

Saba No Misoni (mackerel
simmered with miso), *140,*
141–42

Sakana No Misoyaki (grilled miso-
marinated fish), 102–03, *103*

Sumiso Ae (squid and scallions with
miso-vinegar dressing), 235–36,
237

Tonjiru (hearty miso soup with
pork and vegetables), *80,* 81–82

Miso Shiru (miso soup with tofu), *76,*
77

Misozuke (miso pickles), 243

mushrooms

Dobin Mushi (aromatic "tea pot"
soup with mushrooms, fish, and
shrimp), 89–90, *91*

Karashi Ae (Brussels sprouts,
shrimp, and mushrooms with
mustard dressing), 230–31

Kinoko Zaru Soba (chilled soba
noodles with mushrooms),
184–85

Shira Ae (spinach, carrot, and
shiitake with tofu dressing), *232,*
233–34

musu (to steam), 121

Chawanmushi (egg custard with
shrimp, chicken, and fish), *132,*
133–34, *135*

Sakana No Sakamushi (fish steamed
in kombu with spicy soy sauce),
122, 122–23

Shumai (Japanese-style shrimp
dumplings), *124,* 125–31, *126–29*

N

Nabeyaki Udon ("clay pot" udon
noodle soup), *194,* 195–96

Nasu No Misoyaki (eggplant with
chicken and miso sauce), 104–05

Nikujaga (Japanese-style beef stew),
155–56, *157*

niru (to simmer), 137

Buta No Kakuni (slow-cooked pork
belly with beer-teriyaki glaze),
148–49, 150–51

Chikuzenni (chicken simmered with
lotus root and bamboo shoot),
152, 153–54, *154*

Hambagu (Japanese-style hamburger with tangy sauce), 146–47, *147*

Hijiki (sweet simmered hijiki seaweed), 158, *159*

Karei Raisu (Japanese-style curry), *160*, 161–62

Nikujaga (Japanese-style beef stew), 155–56, *157*

Nitsuke (fish simmered with sake, soy sauce, and sugar), *144*, 145

Oden (Japanese-style hot pot), *164–65*, 166–67

otoshibuta simmering tool, 139

Saba No Misoni (mackerel simmered with miso), *140*, 141–42

Nitsuke (fish simmered with sake, soy sauce, and sugar), *144*, 145

noodle soups. *See also* supu (soups)

Kamo Nanban Soba (soba noodle soup with duck and spring vegetables), 186–87

Nabeyaki Udon ("clay pot" udon noodle soup), *194*, 195–96

noodle stir-fries. *See also* men (noodles)

Kaisen Yaki Udon (stir-fried udon noodles with seafood), 174–75

Yakisoba (stir-fried noodles with pork, cabbage, and ginger), *176*, 177–78, *179*

Nukazuke (rice bran pickles), *244–45*, 246–47

O

Oden (Japanese-style hot pot), *164–65*, 166–67

Ohitashi (dashi-marinated kale), 22

oil, saving, 203

Omuraisu (omelet with ketchup-fried rice), *40*, 40–41

Onigiri (rice balls), *36*, 37–38. *See also* Yaki Onigiri (grilled rice balls)

otoshibuta simmering tool, 139

Oyako Don (chicken and egg rice bowl), *66*, 67–68

P

parsnips

Kinpira (stir-fried parsnip and carrot), *170*, 171–72

pickles

Bread and Beer Pickles, 247

Misozuke (miso pickles), 243

Nukazuke (rice bran pickles), *244–45*, 246–47

Shiozuke (salt pickles), 242

Tataki Kyuri (smashed cucumber pickles), 240, *241*

pork

Buta No Kakuni (slow-cooked pork belly with beer-teriyaki glaze), *148–49*, 150–51

Buta No Shogayaki (pork belly with ginger and onions), 118, *119*

Gyoza (pork and cabbage dumplings), 109–12, *110–11, 113*

Katsu Don (pork cutlet and egg rice bowl), 69

slicing and cooking properly, 119

Tonjiru (hearty miso soup with pork and vegetables), *80*, 81–82

Tonkatsu (Japanese-style fried pork cutlet), *214*, 215–17

pork (*continued*)

    Yakisoba (stir-fried noodles with
        pork, cabbage, and ginger), *176,*
        177–78, 179

potato chips

    Furikake with Shrimp Shells and
        Potato Chips, 34–35, *34–35*

R

rice, 25–28

    Battera (pressed mackerel sushi),
        61–65, *62–63*

    California Temaki, *58,* 59

    Chahan (Japanese-style fried rice),
        46, 47–49

    Chirashi Zushi (scattered sushi), 52

    cooker, buying a, 29

    Donburi (rice bowls), 65

    Hakumai (perfect white rice), *32, 33*

    Katsu Don (pork cutlet and egg rice
        bowl), 69

    Omuraisu (omelet with ketchup-
        fried rice), *40,* 40–41

    Onigiri (rice balls), *36,* 37–38

    Oyako Don (chicken and egg rice
        bowl), *66,* 67–68

    Su Meshi (sushi rice), 50–52, *51*

    Suteki Don (steak rice bowls with
        spicy teriyaki sauce), 70–71

    Takikomi Gohan (dashi-simmered
        rice with vegetables), *42,* 43–44,
        45

    Tekka Don No Poke (Hawaiian
        poke-style tuna rice bowl), *72,*
        73

    Tuna Temaki, Spicy, *55,* 55–56

Ume-Shiso Temaki, 56

Vegetable Temaki, *57,* 57–58

Yaki Onigiri (grilled rice balls), 39

S

Saba No Misoni (mackerel simmered
    with miso), *140,* 141–42

sakajio fish seasoning technique, 101

Sakana No Misoyaki (grilled miso-
    marinated fish), 102–03, *103*

Sakana No Sakamushi (fish steamed in
    kombu with spicy soy sauce),
    122, 122–23

Sake Shioyaki (salt-grilled salmon),
    100, *101*

salmon

    Sake Shioyaki (salt-grilled salmon),
        100, *101*

salt

    Curry Salt, 206

    itazuri technique, 59

    Matcha Salt, 206

    Sake Shioyaki (salt-grilled salmon),
        100, *101*

    Shiozuke (salt pickles), 242

sauces

    Sesame Aioli, *165,* 167

    Shumai Sauce, 131

    Tare No Teriyaki (teriyaki sauce),
        108

    Tempura Sauce, 206

    Tonkatsu Sauce, 217

scallions

    Sumiso Ae (squid and scallions with
        miso-vinegar dressing), 235–36,
        237

Zara Udon (chilled udon noodles with scallions and ginger), 193

seasoning(s)

    Curry Salt, 206

    Furikake with Shrimp Shells and Potato Chips, 34–35, *34–35*

    Matcha Salt, 206

Sesame Aioli, *165,* 167

Shiozuke (salt pickles), 242

Shira Ae (spinach, carrot, and shiitake with tofu dressing), *232, 233–34*

shiso

    Ume-Shiso Temaki, 56

shrimp

    Chawanmushi (egg custard with shrimp, chicken, and fish), *132, 133–34, 135*

    Dobin Mushi (aromatic "tea pot" soup with mushrooms, fish, and shrimp), 89–90, *91*

    Furikake with Shrimp Shells and Potato Chips, 34–35, *34–35*

    Kaki Age (shrimp and vegetable fritters), 208–09, *209*

    Karashi Ae (Brussels sprouts, shrimp, and mushrooms with mustard dressing), 230–31

    Shumai (Japanese-style shrimp dumplings), *124,* 125–31, *126–29*

Shumai (Japanese-style shrimp dumplings), *124,* 125–31, *126–29*

Shumai Sauce, 131

Spicy Tuna Temaki, *55,* 55–56

spinach

    blanching technique, 234

Shira Ae (spinach, carrot, and shiitake with tofu dressing), *232, 233–34*

squash

    Kabocha Korokke (squash croquettes), *220,* 221–22

squid

    Sumiso Ae (squid and scallions with miso-vinegar dressing), 235–36, *237*

stock(s)

    Dashi (dried fish and kelp), 20, *21*

    Kombu Dashi (kelp), 23

Su Meshi (sushi rice), 50–52, *51*

Sumiso Ae (squid and scallions with miso-vinegar dressing), 235–36, *237*

Supagetti No Teriyaki (chicken teriyaki spaghetti), 197–99, *198*

supu (soups), 75. *See also* noodle soups

    Asari No Miso Shiru (miso soup with clams), 78, *79*

    Dango Jiru (Japanese-style chicken and dumpling soup), 86, *87–88*

    Dobin Mushi (aromatic "tea pot" soup with mushrooms, fish, and shrimp), 89–90, *91*

    Miso Shiru (miso soup with tofu), *76, 77*

    Tamago Supu (Japanese egg drop soup), *84, 85*

    Tonjiru (hearty miso soup with pork and vegetables), 80, *81–82*

sushi. *See also* Temaki (hand rolls)

    Battera (pressed mackerel sushi), *60, 61–65, 62–63*

sushi (*continued*)
    Chirashi Zushi (scattered sushi),
        52
    Su Meshi (sushi rice), 50–52, *51*
Suteki Don (steak rice bowls with spicy
    teriyaki sauce), 70–71

T
Takikomi Gohan (dashi-simmered
    rice with vegetables), *42, 43–44,
    45*
Tamago Supu (Japanese egg drop
    soup), *84, 85*
Tamagoyaki (Japanese omelet),
    115–17, *116–17*
Tare No Teriyaki (teriyaki sauce),
    108
Tataki Kyuri (smashed cucumber
    pickles), 240, *241*
Tekka Don No Poke (Hawaiian poke-
    style tuna rice bowl), *72, 73*
Temaki (hand rolls), 53–59, *54*
    California, *58, 59*
    Spicy Tuna, *55,* 55–56
    Ume-Shiso, 56
    Vegetable, *57,* 57–58
tempura
    seasoning for, 206
    Tempura Sauce, 206
    Yasai Tempura (vegetable tempura),
        204, 205–07
teriyaki
    Buta No Kakuni (slow-cooked pork
        belly with beer-teriyaki glaze),
        148–49, 150–51

Supagetti No Teriyaki (chicken
    teriyaki spaghetti), 197–99,
    198
Suteki Don (steak rice bowls with
    spicy teriyaki sauce), 70–71
Tare No Teriyaki (teriyaki sauce),
    108
Tori No Teriyaki (chicken teriyaki),
    106, 107–08
Tsukune No Teriyaki (chicken
    meatballs with teriyaki sauce),
    98–99
tofu
    Miso Shiru (miso soup with tofu),
        76, 77
    Shira Ae (spinach, carrot, and
        shiitake with tofu dressing), *232,*
        233–34
Tonjiru (hearty miso soup with pork
    and vegetables), *80,* 81–82
Tonkatsu (Japanese-style fried pork
    cutlet), *214,* 215–17
Tonkatsu Sauce, 217
Tori No Teriyaki (chicken teriyaki),
    106, 107–08
tsukeru (to pickle), 239
    Bread and Beer Pickles, 247
    Misozuke (miso pickles), 243
    Nukazuke (rice bran pickles),
        244–45, 246–47
    Shiozuke (salt pickles), 242
    Tataki Kyuri (smashed cucumber
        pickles), 240, *241*
Tsukune No Teriyaki (chicken
    meatballs with teriyaki sauce),
    98–99

Tuna Mayo, *38*
Tuna Temaki, Spicy, *55, 55–56*

U
Udon Noodles, Homemade, *188, 189–92, 190–91*
umami flavor, 16
Ume-Shiso Temaki, 56
umeboshi
    Ume-Shiso Temaki, 56

V
Vegetable Temaki, *57, 57–58*

Y
Yaki Onigiri (grilled rice balls), *39. See also* Onigiri (rice balls)
Yakisoba (stir-fried noodles with pork, cabbage, and ginger), *176, 177–78, 179*
Yakitori Party (grilled chicken and vegetable skewers), *94, 95–97*
yaku (to grill, broil, and sear), 93
    Buta No Shogayaki (pork belly with ginger and onions), 118, *119*

Gyoza (pork and cabbage dumplings), 109–12, *110–11, 113*
Nasu No Misoyaki (eggplant with chicken and miso sauce), 104–05
Sakana No Misoyaki (grilled miso-marinated fish), 102–03, *103*
Sake Shioyaki (salt-grilled salmon), 100, *101*
Tamagoyaki (Japanese omelet), 115–17, *116–17*
Tori No Teriyaki (chicken teriyaki), *106,* 107–08
Tsukune No Teriyaki (chicken meatballs with teriyaki sauce), 98–99
Yakitori Party (grilled chicken and vegetable skewers), *94, 95–97*
Yasai Itame (stir-fried vegetables), 173
Yasai Tempura (vegetable tempura), *204, 205–07*

Z
Zaru Udon (chilled udon noodles with scallions and ginger), 193

FIRST EDITION

Photographs © 2016 Evan Sung

Designed by Suet Yee Chong

Library of Congress Cataloging-in-Publication Data has been
applied for.

ISBN 978-0-06-234438-0

17 18 19 20   OV/QGT   10 9 8 7 6 5 4 3